Praise for
ENVY: THE ENEMY
WITHIN

Bob Sorge has not only unearthed but has also helped us to
overcome one of Christendom's greatest deterrents to fruitfulness:
envy. This will be a must-read for every vigilant leader who desires
to make a difference within his or her lifetime. This message
will save you 10 years of unnecessary pain!

Dr. Wayne Cordeiro
New Hope Christian Fellowship

This book reminds us how deep and far our sin can reach, and it
also gets us on track toward freedom. The journey is difficult, but
Bob Sorge has given us excellent tools to help along the way.

Ted Haggard
Author, *The Life-Giving Church*
Senior Pastor, New Life Church
Colorado Springs, Colorado

This book could not have come at a better time. Seemingly at every
level of society we are seeing this insidious sin. Bob Sorge has a word
from the Lord to rescue the Church from the poison of envy.

John A. Kilpatrick
Senior Pastor, Brownsville Assembly of God Church
Pensacola, Florida

Envy: The Enemy Within is a book filled with scriptural exposition on the topic and keen insight into human nature and relationship. Although we might be reluctant to acknowledge it, what the author writes about is a shoe that fits all of us in one way or another. And since he spends a good amount of time addressing the problem within the Church, those of us in ministry might find it an especially good fit.

Ron Mehl
AUTHOR, *GOD WORKS THE NIGHT SHIFT* AND *THE TENDER COMMANDMENTS*
PASTOR, BEAVERTON FOURSQUARE CHURCH
BEAVERTON, OREGON

Only a broken but bold vessel could write a book like *Envy: The Enemy Within*. In this book Bob Sorge represents God's heart to lead His people out of captivity and into freedom. This is probably one of the greatest displays of revelation I have read in the last 10 years. If the Body of Christ removes envy, strife and jealousy, we will quit warring with each other, become the worshipers God created us to be and overthrow the enemy's plan against God's kingdom advancement. This book takes you to the Cross and into resurrection power. *Envy: The Enemy Within* is one of the few books that I can honestly say will revolutionize your life. Once this evil force is removed from us, the glory of God will move in our midst!

Dr. Chuck D. Pierce
AUTHOR, *THE FUTURE WAR OF THE CHURCH*
VICE PRESIDENT, GLOBAL HARVEST MINISTRIES
PRESIDENT, GLORY OF ZION INTERNATIONAL, INC.

In Acts 6 there is an account of how the leaders of the Early Church dealt with envy. The Greek-speaking Jews thought that the widows of the Hebrew-speaking Jews were receiving a more favorable distribution of food. Their perception could have wreaked havoc within the young movement. However, the spiritual wisdom of the apostles created a plan that nipped envy at the root, and the growth of the Church continued. Bob Sorge has brought the same spiritual wisdom to today's challenge of envy. Reading this manuscript will help us see where envy has crept into our lives and into the Church and how it is hindering the work of the Church in the earth today. Bob also shares that this doesn't have to be the case. There is a way to root out envy and move forward in love.

Pastor Dutch Sheets
Author, *Intercessory Prayer* and *Tell Your Heart to Beat Again*
Pastor, Spring Harvest Fellowship
Colorado Springs, Colorado

E N V Y
the enemy within

BOB SORGE

Regal

From Gospel Light
Ventura, California, U.S.A.

PUBLISHED BY REGAL BOOKS
FROM GOSPEL LIGHT
VENTURA, CALIFORNIA, U.S.A.
PRINTED IN THE U.S.A.

Regal

Regal Books is a ministry of Gospel Light, an evangelical Christian publisher dedicated to serving the local church. We believe God's vision for Gospel Light is to provide church leaders with biblical, user-friendly materials that will help them evangelize, disciple and minister to children, youth and families.

It is our prayer that this Regal book will help you discover biblical truth for your own life and help you meet the needs of others. May God richly bless you.

For a free catalog of resources from Regal Books/Gospel Light, please call your Christian supplier or contact us at 1-800-4-GOSPEL *or* www.regalbooks.com.

Cover and interior design by Robert Williams
Edited by Deena Davis

LIBRARY OF CONGRESS CATALOGING-IN-PUBLICATION DATA
Sorge, Bob.
    Envy : the enemy within / Bob Sorge.
        p. cm.
    ISBN 0-8307-3122-9
    1. Envy—Religious aspects—Christianity. 2. Jealousy—Religious
aspects—Christianity. I. Title.
    BV4627.E5 S66 2003
    241'.4—dc21   2002151156

1   2   3   4   5   6   7   8   9   10   11   12   13   14   15   /   09   08   07   06   05   04   03

Rights for publishing this book in other languages are contracted by Gospel Light World-wide, the international nonprofit ministry of Gospel Light. Gospel Light Worldwide also provides publishing and technical assistance to international publishers dedicated to producing Sunday School and Vacation Bible School curricula and books in the languages of the world. For additional information, visit www.gospellightworldwide.org; write to Gospel Light Worldwide, P.O. Box 3875, Ventura, CA 93006; or send an e-mail to info@gospellightworldwide.org.

CONTENTS

Chapter 1 9

The Most Common Problem That Nobody Has

It's time to stop calling envy everyone else's problem. Let's demystify it and own up to the truth.

Chapter 2 17

What Is Envy?

Whenever we feel pain over another's success, envy has us in its diabolically deadly claws.

Chapter 3 28

The Brothers

Envy is usually an issue between brothers—and sisters. We can trace that pattern beginning with Cain and Abel and continue on through biblical history.

Chapter 4 45

The Great Talent Showdown

When God gives out varying degrees of talent, it's a masterfully designed setup for an envy eruption.

Chapter 5 67

Why Revival Tarries

Could it be that envy is the most formidable hindrance to true biblical revival?

Chapter 6 77

The Cross: Death of Envy

God deals with envy by crucifying the one who is envied—the foremost example being Jesus.

Chapter 7 90

Perceiving the "Measure of Grace"

As we explore comparison and the seemingly arbitrary distribution of spiritual gifts and different spheres of influence, there are things we can do to overcome envy.

Chapter 8 115

The Envy Detour: Death or Destiny

When God wants to bless a person or a ministry, He minimizes the envy factor by taking them to their promised land via a circuitous, arduous detour.

Chapter 9 132

Rooted in Love

At the heart of envy is the issue of love and the need to be rooted in Christ's love as the source of our personal identity.

CHAPTER 1

THE MOST COMMON PROBLEM THAT NOBODY HAS

I HAVE A PROBLEM WITH ENVY—a *huge* problem with envy. Because *any* problem with envy is a huge problem. Envy runs so deep in the inner recesses of my carnal flesh that it's probably a whole lot worse than I realize. (Who of us knows our own heart?) This book exists simply because God has had to speak *volumes* to me about the envy of my heart.

My own struggles with envy are rooted in a certain competitiveness that seems native to my personality or upbringing. I don't know why—I just know I've been competitive all my life. Whether it was a sports event or a board game or a scholastic assignment,

I have always been motivated to perform at my best. While the pursuit of excellence can be praiseworthy when it's submitted to Christ's Lordship, I've discovered that the desire to excel beyond my friends can actually be the seedbed for envious heart attitudes. When I stepped into the arena of Kingdom ministry, the old ambitious desires didn't completely fall away, even though I told myself they had. When I saw my friends enjoying successes that I desired for myself, envy quietly sulked below the surface. (Envy is the internal pain we feel over someone else's success—but we'll define it more clearly in the next chapter.)

I didn't see my envy for a long time. But when God started to reveal it to me, I was appalled at what I saw of the true condition of my heart. Now I am fervently committed to radical repentance and walking in the light in this area of my life.

I am compelled to honestly share my own shortcomings in the area of envy for two reasons. Firstly, I've learned the power of the flesh is amazingly broken when we bring our sins into the light (see John 1:7; James 5:16), so I gladly receive the grace that comes to me through the humility of confession. Scripture tells us that "God resists the proud, but gives grace to the humble" (James 4:6). I need that grace more desperately than I could possibly say. Secondly, I want to assure you that I'm not speaking from the aloof position of someone who is beyond envy's tentacles. I am still in process of victory. I hope you can receive the message of this book from a fellow pilgrim who is even yet in this journey with God.

WHY THIS BOOK

As the Lord has challenged the envious tendencies of my soul, I have come to realize how pandemic envy truly is and how deadly it is every time it infects the church of Jesus Christ. Envy has the power to sabotage our own personal destiny in God because God cannot honor our efforts when they are subliminally driven by impure motives. As long as envy remains hidden in the crevices of our hearts, our fruitfulness in Christ will inescapably be impeded.

But more than that—and here's where I sense an even greater urgency—when we envy one another in the kingdom of God, we release dynamics that actually bind the progress of the Kingdom

eNVY kiLLeD tHe BODY of Jesus CHRist WHEN He came to tHis pLaNet tHe fiRst time, aND it's stiLL kiLLiNG His BODY toDay.

in our sphere, or region. Envy has the power to obstruct the release of Kingdom blessing, even in places where massive amounts of intercession for revival and visitation are ascending to God's throne. In fact, I will argue in this book that envy has been responsible, perhaps more than any other evil or vice, for quenching the fires of revival both in the past and in the present.

Envy killed the body of Jesus Christ when He came to this planet the first time, and it's still killing His body—the church— today. I pray that this book will be read by every saint—by the youth, by the elderly, by ministers, by servants and by believers of all tribes and denominations. The Spirit is sounding a clarion call in this critical hour that we understand what envy is, perceive it in our own hearts and know how to cooperate with God's grace so that this evil leech will stop sapping us of the Holy Spirit power we need to complete the task of global evangelization.

Perhaps you feel baffled, or even offended, that this little book would even *suggest* that you might have a problem with envy. Oh, how easily our hearts deceive us! We are so prone to think more highly of ourselves than we ought (see Romans 12:3; Philippians 2:3). Now please understand that I do not write this book from a spirit of accusation. Rather, it is my desire to bring the real issues surrounding envy into the light and then point the way toward healing and freedom in Christ.

I believe it is time for the body of Christ to wake up to the reality of envy and what it is doing to us. Let's own the truth: It's *my* problem; it's *our* problem. Envy is alive and well in the church of Jesus Christ, and it is wreaking havoc throughout the body as it impedes the progress of God's glorious kingdom. Let's launch this discussion by speaking the truth in our hearts (see Psalm 15:2) about our true state of affairs. It's time to lower our defenses and ask God to speak to us personally about this subject.

This isn't a book only to recommend to others; it is a book whose message we need to apply to our own lives. As the old song says, "Not my brother, not my sister, but it's me, O Lord, standing in the need of prayer."

If your first response is, "Envy? Not a problem for me, as best I can tell," then let me make an appeal to you: Read this short book anyway. You will not simply be educated to the nature and ramifications of envy. More than that, your vision of God's purposes for the church will be enlarged, and you will see why the Holy Spirit is strategically highlighting the issue of envy among believers today. It is of paramount importance that we gain our inheritance in Christ! If we will heed the Spirit's voice regarding envy and how it fractures the body of Christ, then this generation has the potential to see the power and glory of God manifest in the earth in an unprecedented manner.

ENVY IS EVERYWHERE

We are surrounded today by envy at every turn. About a month after the September 11, 2001 collapse of New York City's twin towers, our local newspaper carried an interesting column that reflected international anger toward the United States. Americans were surprised by some of the sentiments of people from other nations:

"Americans have had it coming for a long time," said a Canadian.

"The thug got beat up," is how one Moscow metalworker put it.

Newspaper columnist Rick Montgomery editorialized, "We were aghast: How could radical Muslims dance while thousands of innocents lay dead beneath the rubble of the World Trade Center?" The columnist went on to suggest that international criticism of the United States was based on the supposition that America is "the symbol of all that is big." Montgomery's analysis was that "military and economic triumphs here have bred envy and scorn elsewhere."[1]

Montgomery's analysis carries a measure of validity. While envy is not the only contributing factor to such tensions, it certainly is a tangible part. There are some in other nations who rejoice over any outbreak of calamity in America because of their envy of America's strengths.

There is good reason to connect the current tensions in the Middle East with the envy-induced parting of ways that happened between Isaac and Ishmael almost 4,000 years ago. (Because he envied the favor granted to his brother, Ishmael mocked Isaac and was cast out of the house by Isaac's mother, Sarah.) The ripple effect of the envy between those two brothers is still being felt today through their various descendants, most specifically in today's Israeli-Arab conflicts. Could it be possible that envy is linked, at least in part, to virtually every ethnic and religious war on the face of our planet today? My point in a sentence is this: Our world is *filled* with envy!

However, space won't permit us to deal with the many forms of envy in the world today. The scope of this book is to look at envy within the ranks of the church of Jesus Christ. We won't be looking at how someone might envy another's car or house, spouse, children, good looks, career or financial status. Rather, we're going to narrow our focus to the specter of envy that rises between Christian brothers and sisters and their differing ministries. Between my church and your church. Between my anointing and your anointing. Between my ministry and your ministry.

DO WE HAVE TO USE THE E WORD?

There's something fundamentally distressing about confessing to the E word ("envy"). A friend recently told me how the Holy Spirit was convicting him about envy, and it took him several days of wrestling with God before he could say, "Okay, Lord, I'm willing to admit it. I'm envious. Forgive me."

Maybe one reason we don't want to call it envy is because we would like to think we've grown beyond the carnality of the believers in Corinth, to whom Paul had to write a stern rebuke for their comparisons between various ministers.

> I fed you with milk and not with solid food; for until now you were not able to receive it, and even now you are still not able; for you are still carnal. For where there are envy, strife, and divisions among you, are you not carnal and behaving like mere men? For when one says, "I am of Paul," and another, "I am of Apollos," are you not carnal? (1 Corinthians 3:2-4).

We resist pinning the label "envy" on the struggles of our soul because of the implications that word carries with it. If we own up to envy, we are giving admittance to some powerfully indicting weaknesses. We are tacitly admitting the following attitudes:

• I am not fully established and at rest in my identity in Christ.

- I have insecurities that have not been fully healed through the power of His grace.
- I am ungrateful for what God has given me. His gifts are not enough for me; I also want what He's given another.
- I am striving against God's sovereignty and wisdom by questioning His giving differing gifts and endowments of grace to both me and my brother or sister.
- My heart is motivated at a fundamental level by an element of self-interest, self-preservation and self-promotion. I am not able to fully celebrate my brother's successes because of underlying feelings of competition and ambition in my soul.
- When all my energies should be focused upon the war against the enemy of our souls, some of my energy has been diverted to struggling over the successes of my fellow believers.
- Since envy, when it is full grown, culminates in murder, I have the seeds of murder within my heart.
- My carnality is impeding the unity of the body of Christ—the unity that is central to the bride's preparation. Hence, part of me is hindering, instead of hastening, Christ's return.

When God began to show me the envy of my heart, at first I was shocked. But I'm long since over that. Now, it never surprises me when I discover it afresh. *Oh, it's that old ugly thing again, is it?* The Holy Spirit seems especially committed to highlighting it to me. He shows it to me when it's in its budding stage so that I can repent early. I'm not sure how much progress I've gained over envy, but I do know I've become a faster repenter. So when I look at the list above, it has become very easy for me to confess, "Yup, guilty as charged." I'm no longer shocked, because I've been given a revelation of the iniquitous potential of my flesh.

Here is what I've discovered: *When envy becomes easy to confess, victory comes within closer reach.*

Envy doesn't have to be full grown to be present. Envy can appear in our hearts in its most preliminary stages, and it can also develop into full maturity if we refuse to deal with it. All of

WHEN ENVY BECOMES EASY TO CONFESS, VICTORY COMES WITHIN CLOSER REACH.

us are tempted to envy. To be tempted is not in and of itself sinful (see Hebrews 4:15). But it's also true that most, if not all, of us have succumbed to envy at some point in our lives. In other words, we're dealing with a *universal* problem.

I remember reading of a poll among Christians where the respondents agreed that envy is primarily a sin among women. As a male writer, I have one word for that survey finding: *Preposterous!* It is a major issue for *all* of us. (They must have polled some delusional males.) Envy is one of the most fundamental by-products of our fallen human condition, and it's been with every generation since Cain and Abel. Little wonder that Jesus devoted some of His most powerful parables directly to this topic (see Matthew 20 and 25).

May the Lord empower us with the courage and understanding to hear what the Spirit is saying to the church in this regard. Let's begin by asking the question, What is envy?

Note

1. Rick Montgomery, "Anger Takes Americans by Surprise," *Kansas City Star* (October 15, 2001), n.p.

Chapter 2

WHAT IS ENVY?

I remember a leading secular magazine once defined envy as the pain felt when someone has what you want. We know from Scripture that that pain is, in fact, a sinful desire (see Galatians 5:21,26). *Vine's Expository Dictionary* has defined envy as "the feeling of displeasure produced by witnessing or hearing of the advantage or prosperity of others."[1] *Webster's Dictionary* defines envy as "the painful or resentful awareness of an advantage enjoyed by another joined with a desire to possess the same advantage."[2] It's the pain or distress we feel over another's success. The meaning of the word "jealousy" is slightly different from envy. *Webster's* defines "jealous" as "disposed to suspect rivalry or unfaithfulness; hostile toward a rival or one believed to enjoy an advantage."[3]

In many contexts the words "envy" and "jealousy" are virtually interchangeable. There are shades of meaning that are unique to each word, but those differences are not really important to the purpose of this book. It could be argued that jealousy is my attitude about *what I have*, while envy is my attitude about *what another has*. There are a variety of definitions out there, such as, "The distinction lies in this, that envy desires to deprive another of what he has; jealousy desires to have the same or the same sort of thing for itself."[4] Such distinction seems somewhat artificial to me. "Envy" and "jealousy" are very similar in meaning, but "envy" seems to be the darker word. When confessing sin, I follow the policy of describing my sin in its worst possible terms. So I will use the word "envy" in this book.

Like most emotions, envy and jealousy have both a positive and negative side. There is a balanced jealousy that guards an exclusive, covenantal relationship (such as marriage). God is so jealous for our affections that He even calls Himself by the name Jealous (see Exodus 34:14). Furthermore, James 4:5 speaks of the jealousy (the actual word is literally "envy") of the Holy Spirit as He yearns for our undivided loyalties. So there is an envy that can be good when it is directed properly. But that is the only Scripture that puts envy in a positive light. All other references point to envy as a carnal desire of the flesh.

Envy derives from our carnal, fleshly self-life. Its source is within the human heart (see Mark 7:21-23). In listing the works of the flesh, Paul includes both envy and jealousy:

> Now the works of the flesh are evident, which are: adultery, fornication, uncleanness, lewdness, idolatry, sorcery, hatred, contentions, *jealousies*, outbursts of wrath, selfish ambitions, dissensions, heresies, *envy*, murders, drunkenness, revelries, and the like; of which I tell you beforehand, just as I also told you in time past, that those who practice such things will not inherit the kingdom of God (Galatians 5:19-21, emphasis added).

There is no denying the obvious parallels between envy and the tenth commandment, which reads, "You shall not covet your neighbor's house; you shall not covet your neighbor's wife, nor his male servant, nor his female servant, nor his ox, nor his donkey, nor anything that is your neighbor's" (Exodus 20:17). Christian apologist Francis Schaeffer believed that in our fallenness the tenth commandment is always the first one we break, before any of the other nine. Our tendency to envy is so fundamental to our fallen identity that God chose to address it from the start—in the Ten Commandments.

THE DOWNSIDE OF SUCCESS

Whether the feeling originates in your heart toward another or comes against you from another, envy is the backlash of diligence. For example, when you're diligent to gain excellence in a given field of endeavor, others who also aspire to that same field are aroused to jealousy by your attainments. To say it another

ENVY IS THE BACKLASH OF DILIGENCE.

way, those who climb the ladder of success faster are envied by the other climbers. Solomon pointed to this when he wrote, "Again, I saw that for all toil and every skillful work a man is envied by his neighbor. This also is vanity and grasping for the wind" (Ecclesiastes 4:4). Solomon's conclusion was that the community's negative response to a diligent man's attainments is one of the fundamental curses of our human existence.

Pastor Michael Cavanaugh expressed it this way: "Envy is the natural by-product of being favored by God."[5] When God chooses you for blessing, just get ready for the downside, because envy from other people is one of the "occupational hazards" of receiving God's blessing. As the proverb goes, It's the tallest tree that gets hit by lightning. Those who stand out among their brethren often come under attack. Many times envy will seem to be almost irrational and unreasonable—coming at you seemingly out of left field—but it's the common experience of those who have been chosen by God for particular gifting and usefulness and anointing.

Sociologists have coined the term "limited good" to describe a commonly held presupposition that there is only so much honor and prosperity and success available to the citizens of a society at any given time. So for one citizen to increase in success, he must of necessity take from the success of others in that society. Envy, they say, is thus the natural response of citizens in a society who—when looking upon the success of someone—realize that success has come to that person at their own expense and loss. This idea—that there is only so much to go around—is not to be found in the kingdom of God, however, because the resources of God toward His children are lavishly boundless and extravagantly plentiful. Unfortunately, our sinful nature tends to carry the baggage of unsanctified thought patterns into our new life in Christ.

THE BOOK OF JAMES ON ENVY

Perhaps the most compelling New Testament passage on envy is found in the book of James.

> But if you have bitter envy and self-seeking in your hearts, do not boast and lie against the truth. This wisdom does not descend from above, but is earthly, sensual, demonic. For where envy and self-seeking exist, confusion and every evil thing are there. But the wisdom that is from above is first pure, then peaceable, gentle, willing to yield, full of

mercy and good fruits, without partiality and without hypocrisy (James 3:14-17).

James tells us that envy is "bitter." It is empowered by an embittered heart and produces bitter fruit in relationships. An example of that is found in the life of Esau (see Genesis 27). When it came time for Esau to receive the patriarchal blessing from his father Isaac, Esau's twin brother, Jacob, put on his brother's clothes and pretended to be Esau. Trying to imitate Esau's voice, Jacob went to his father and deceptively stole the

envy's energies are generated from a self-seeking heart of personal ambition.

blessing that Isaac had intended for Esau. When Jacob got the blessing that Esau deserved as the firstborn, Esau's eye turned evil toward his brother. Esau was caught in the grip of envy, but he felt justified in his bitterness toward his brother, Jacob, because Jacob had wronged him. Envy can produce a root of bitterness in someone's heart, which, if not dealt with, can eventually defile many people (see Hebrews 12:15-16). Therefore, when we are envious, we should ask ourselves why we are bitter. If we are honest, most of our bitterness is probably directed against God, because He is the One who has given more to others than to us.

James also connects envy with self-seeking. Envy and self-seeking shadow each other. Envy's energies are generated from a self-seeking heart of personal ambition. Because of our sin nature, we are motivated at the core of our being by selfish ambitions. Ambition can be turned for good in the Kingdom, but it requires a torturous crucifixion before the self-serving elements of ambition are driven completely from us. The apostle Paul was a man who harnessed the ambitious tendencies of his soul and turned them into a passionate pursuit of "the upward call of God in Christ Jesus" (Philippians 3:14). And yet, while ambition can be properly directed into a pursuit of the Kingdom, virtually all of us have to struggle with the negative elements of ambition and self-seeking that cause us to envy others.

James goes on to say that envy will "boast and lie against the truth." Because envy is rooted in pride, it will easily lead to boasting about oneself. When in the presence of someone who has been given more than us, envy will want us to advertise our own merits. But such boasting usually comes from an inflated opinion of ourselves. So instead of speaking the truth about ourselves, we lie against the truth of who we are and what we have.

The source of envy and boasting, James tells us, is not from above. Rather, he ascribes a threefold source to this kind of envy. It is earthly (rooted in the natural realm); it is sensual (based on data received from the five senses rather than from the Spirit of God); and it is demonic (inflamed by demonic activity).

Then James delivers this chilling summary: "For where envy and self-seeking exist, confusion and every evil thing are there." What a mouthful! We'll return to that statement before we're done.

ENVY AND STRIFE

Just as self-seeking shadows envy, so does strife. Strife is a contention between people, a struggle for superiority. Strife is often (although not always) motivated by envy. We see this in the very first mention of strife in the Bible. Abram's herdsmen and Lot's herdsmen were striving with each other over pasture land for their livestock (see Genesis 13:7-8). Even though Lot was amply provided for, it seems that he envied Abram's abundant blessings.

Lot's attitude filtered down to his herdsmen, and they began to contend for the best feeding grounds. Abram stepped forward to diffuse the strife by accepting the inferior pastureland.

Strife is positioned with *envy* in five New Testament verses:

Being filled with all unrighteousness, sexual immorality, wickedness, covetousness, maliciousness; full of envy, murder, strife (Romans 1:29; see also 2 Corinthians 12:20).

Let us walk properly, as in the day, not in revelry and drunkenness, not in lewdness and lust, not in strife and envy (Romans 13:13).

Some indeed preach Christ even from envy and strife (Philippians 1:15).

He is proud, knowing nothing, but is obsessed with disputes and arguments over words, from which come envy, strife, reviling, evil suspicions (1 Timothy 6:4).

We can clearly see from these Scriptures that strife and envy operate hand in hand.

In the first chapter of Philippians, Paul discusses the motives of the preachers of the gospel in his day. He points to two general groups of preachers, each group driven by opposite motivations.

Some indeed preach Christ even from envy and strife, and some also from goodwill: The former preach Christ from selfish ambition, not sincerely, supposing to add affliction to my chains; but the latter out of love, knowing that I am appointed for the defense of the gospel. What then? Only that in every way, whether in pretense or in truth,

Christ is preached; and in this I rejoice, yes, and will rejoice
(Philippians 1:15-18).

Paul recognized that the zeal of some ministers was fueled by
envy and strife. They were not energized by a fire of holy love for
the beautiful Son of God but by a desire to promote their own
ministry. Paul could not be bought or manipulated, so they perceived him as a threat to their success. Therefore they tried to
discredit Paul, most likely by saying despicable things about his
chains and reputation as a criminal. If they could poison the
guards with suspicious thoughts, the guards would treat Paul
more severely. Their envy moved them to step on Paul in their
attempts to climb the ministry ladder.

Like James, Paul linked envy with selfish ambition. "Selfish
ambition" is just one word in the original text, the Greek word
eritheia. It is a very colorful word that evolved in its meaning to
describe a hireling (someone working for pay). It described someone who was concerned only with his own welfare—a person who
was susceptible to being bribed. Eritheia pictured an ambitious,
self-willed person seeking opportunities for promotion.

The opposite motivation for preaching the gospel was "out
of love." When we are released from envy, we can serve the Lord
with a pure heart of love for Him, for His servants, for His people and for the lost.

TWO DREAMS

Chris Berglund (a friend who lives in Kansas City) told me of two
dreams he had which carried spiritual significance for him—and
may be meaningful for some of us too. He has given me permis-
sion to repeat his story in the hope that it might help someone
else gain freedom in the same area. At the time the dreams came
he was pastor of a small church in Seattle, Washington. In the

first dream, Chris saw himself in a church meeting where the guest speaker called him by name and said, "Chris, the Lord says you have a life-threatening disease." Chris was shocked by the news and began to wonder if he had cancer. The speaker then added, "The life-threatening disease you have is Comparison." Chris's first response was, *I don't agree with this,* and yet he knew it was somehow true.

For the next three days Chris struggled to understand the meaning of the dream. He had worked so hard for years to bless others, to not judge others, etc. How could he be diseased with Comparison? But then understanding suddenly came. Chris told me, "For years I had compared myself to others and always ended up on the shorter end of the stick. The Lord brought to my remembrance all the times I had said to myself, *Why teach? Mike Bickle is such a better teacher. Why prophesy? Paul Cain seems to have the market on that. Why pray? Lou Engle has so much more fire than I do when he prays.* Chris said he kept comparing himself with others and fell short, and it was killing his spiritual life in God.

The follow-up dream, which came a few weeks later, was to emphasize what God wanted Chris to learn. In this dream Chris was in the mountains with a group of men he had always respected because of the strength of the Holy Spirit's anointing upon their ministries. Each one, he felt, was more effective than himself in their respective areas of ministry. They each had their own private cabins, but they gathered at a main meeting hall that had a table set for meals. The honored guest for the weekend was Billy Graham, and he was just about to arrive. All were gathered around the table when Billy Graham arrived and walked up to Chris and said, "Chris, I would like to sit by you tonight for dinner." Chris replied, "No, you don't really want to sit with me; you want to sit with this one or that one. I'm boring compared to these guys." But Billy proceeded to pull out a chair next to Chris. After dinner he said, "Chris, I would like to sleep in your cabin tonight." Again

Chris remonstrated, "My cabin is a mess." But Billy acted like he didn't hear and he joined Chris in his cabin. Upon entering, Billy began cleaning and tidying the cabin.

Here's how Chris told me he interpreted the dream: "I knew when I woke that Billy Graham represented the Lord. He was showing me how much He loved me for who I am—even in my weakness. He was continuing to break Comparison off me, so I could see that His love for me wasn't based on my giftedness and works, or lack thereof. He simply wanted to be with me."

The dreams sparked a time of powerful spiritual encounter for Chris as the Lord began the process of delivering him, layer by layer, from the deadly disease of Comparison.

THE POTENCY OF ENVY

Envy is a powerful passion. God's Word says that "a sound heart is life to the body, but envy is rottenness to the bones" (Proverbs 14:30). In some cases envy festers inside as a quiet comparing of ourselves with others or an inner resentment. Sometimes it finds expression as a root of bitterness that moves beyond the individual and begins to defile the many. And in other cases it ends in outright murder. For example, it was envy that caused the religious leaders to crucify our Lord Jesus (see Matthew 27:18).

Envy is like a seedling. It may start off as a small seed, but if it is harbored and nursed, it will eventually grow into a tree of evil. In its ripest form, envy is a spirit of murder and robbery, for ultimately it wants to kill and then apprehend the coveted possession for itself.

Author and Bible teacher Bob Mumford has referred to envy as "a crab bucket mentality." He said you never have to put a lid on a crab bucket because they'll never allow each other to escape.

Jesus taught His disciples to give alms in secret and to pray in secret and to fast in secret, because in all three cases He repeated this consequence: "And your Father who sees in secret will Himself reward you openly" (Matthew 6:4; see also vv. 6,18). When these instructions are followed by believers, they are a guaranteed recipe for breeding envy in others. What you do in secret is seen by nobody but your Father in heaven; but when He rewards you openly, the rewards are seen by men. Men don't see the price you paid; they only see the dividends received. When they see you being rewarded openly, they don't understand what you've been sowing in secret, so their first response is envy. When a brother sees another brother getting blessed for no obvious reason, often the carnal nature wants to respond with envy.

Envy is as old as Cain and Abel. But to go there we need to go to the next chapter.

Notes

1. W. E. Vine, *Vine's Expository Dictionary of New Testament Words* (Iowa Falls, IA: Riverside Book and Bible House), p. 367.
2. *Merriam-Webster's Collegiate Dictionary,* 10th ed., s.v. "envy."
3. Ibid., s.v. "jealous."
4. W. E. Vine, *Vine's Expository Dictionary,* p. 367.
5. Michael Cavanaugh, *A Study in Envy—Saul and David,* audiotape of teaching by Michael Cavanaugh presented at Elim Gospel Church, Lima, New York, January 21, 2001.

CHAPTER 3

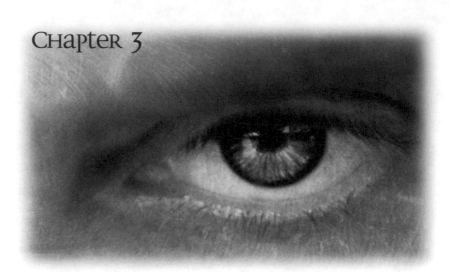

THE BROTHERS

ENVY SURFACED RIGHT at the BEGINNING of HUMAN HISTORY, with Cain and Abel (Adam's two sons). Cain envied Abel because Abel's sacrifice was acceptable to God, and Cain's was not. Even before Cain killed his brother, God warned him, "Sin lies at the door. And its desire is for you, but you should rule over it" (Genesis 4:7). The sin crouching at the door of Cain's heart was envy. Either he would master it or it would master him. Sadly, envy won. Cain murdered his brother Abel.

Envy is always an issue of *the brothers*. The only reason envy didn't start with Adam is because Adam had no brother. But as soon as brothers appeared on the earth, envy immediately sprang to life. Envy is usually not an issue between father and son but between brothers (and, as we will see in a moment, between sisters).

A true father does not envy his son, and a true son does not envy his father. Absalom was not a true son to David, so he envied his father's domain. But Timothy and Titus were "true sons" to Paul (see 1 Timothy 1:2; Titus 1:4), so they never envied Paul's sphere of ministry, realizing that in honoring their spiritual father's sphere they would come into far greater blessings than if they attempted to usurp it.

By saying that envy is an issue among brothers, I mean more than just natural siblings. I'm talking about those who serve side by side in the same general sphere of influence. So the members of a home group would be brothers, and the home-group leader would be the father in that context. At the next sphere of influence, the home-group leaders of a local church would be brothers to each other (whether male or female), and the pastor would be their father. The pastors of a city would in turn be brothers to each other (whether male or female), while someone like a Billy Graham would be viewed by those pastors as a father.

envy is an iniquity of the heart that is not seen until an occasion calls it forth.

Home-group leaders usually don't envy the successes of their pastor—rather, they gain momentum from the success of their pastor. But the success of another home-group leader? That's another matter entirely. Since the other home-group leader operates in the same ministry sphere, the flesh wants to perceive the other brother as competition.

Envy is an iniquity of the heart that is not seen until an occasion calls it forth. So until the occasion comes along, we can be sincerely convinced that envy is not an issue of struggle for us. But God knows how to help us see the envying tendencies of our hearts (so that we can do business with Him and repent). His most common method of revealing our tendencies to envy is to pour out blessings on one of our brothers.

While my brother was struggling, I found I could pray for him with energy and sincerity. But when the blessing of God exploded around his life, something else exploded within my heart, and I could no longer pray for him as in former times. God had answered my prayer by blessing my brother, and now my pity had turned to envy.

THE SISTERS

Envy is also an issue among *the sisters*. The sisters usually don't envy the "mothers" in Israel, but it certainly is tempting to envy each other.

Curiously, envy seems to follow gender lines. The brothers envy the brothers and the sisters envy the sisters. There may be the occasional exception, but it's not much of an issue between genders.

CURIOUSLy, eNVy seems to foLLow ġeNDeR LiNes.

The sisters will envy each other for such things as physical appearance, popularity and social status, children and ministry giftings. (The brothers will envy each other for such things as career accomplishments, financial clout, as well as ministry giftings.) Some of the issues are different between genders, but the temptation to envy is equally present.

Envy is often rooted in a struggle to gain identity. When Jacob married the sisters Rachel and Leah and when Leah bore children but Rachel did not, the Scripture says, "Rachel envied her sister, and said to Jacob, 'Give me children, or else I die!'"

(Genesis 30:1). Back in those days, so much of a wife's self-esteem was wrapped up in her ability to produce children for her husband. The envy between the sisters was so strong that God later placed this precept in the Law of Moses: "Nor shall you take a woman as a rival to her sister, to uncover her nakedness while the other is alive" (Leviticus 18:18).

Actually, envy between sisters goes back two generations before Rachel and Leah. Envy was the issue between Sarah and Hagar. Sarah (Abraham's wife) was barren; so in an attempt to have a child, she gave her maidservant Hagar to Abraham as a wife. Hagar bore Ishmael to Abraham, but then her relationship with Sarah suddenly changed from that of a maidservant to that of a rival. Isaac, the miracle baby, was born against the backdrop of a fascinating saga of envy played out by two women who each longed to find her identity in the family as a fruitful mother.

Miriam, Moses' sister, was not envious of Moses; but she did become envious of Moses' wife! Moses' wife, Zipporah, was a Gentile, and Miriam became resentful of the position Zipporah enjoyed as Moses' wife, even though she was not an Israelite (see Numbers 12:1). We don't know the exact nature of her envy; but again, it was among sisters—those functioning in similar spheres of influence. Aaron got caught up in Miriam's emulation, perhaps because he may have envied his brother, Moses. But it's obvious that Miriam was the instigator, because she was the one God struck with leprosy.

And then there was the case of Hannah and Peninnah, the two wives of Elkanah. Peninnah had children, but Hannah was barren. Hannah struggled with envy toward Peninnah because she had children, but Peninnah envied Hannah because Hannah was Elkanah's favorite wife. The consequent tension in the family was almost unbearable. We're told that Peninnah provoked Hannah "severely, to make her miserable, because the LORD had closed her womb" (1 Samuel 1:6). The story ended on a happier note when God enabled Hannah to become pregnant with Samuel.

All these stories among sisters share the common element of two women struggling to become secure in their identity as a wife, mother or sister. Envy is clearly as tempting for the sisters as it is for the brothers. The Bible gives us more examples of envy among brothers than sisters, however, so let's return to look at the brothers.

THE FIRE OF ENVY

In Numbers 16, we read the account of Korah and a band of Levites and leaders in Israel who rallied a demonstration against Moses and Aaron, primarily because they thought Aaron should not be given exclusive rights to be the high priest. They were sons of Levi, just like Aaron, and as brothers within Levi's tribe they became envious because God had sovereignly chosen Aaron over them. The way God punished their envy was sensationally dramatic and terrifying. The ground opened up beneath the feet of the leaders of the rebellion and swallowed them and their entire households alive. Then fire went out from the Lord and consumed the 250 leaders who were participating in the insurrection. Envy had kindled a fire in the camp, and God had to purge it from the camp with His own fire.

The drama of the live burial and deadly fire served to highlight God's attitude toward envy. It's as though God were saying, "This fiery slaughter illustrates how I feel when you envy what I have sovereignly given to another, because in so doing you despise that which I have given to you."

The history of God's covenant people is laden with envy-laced stories. Lot's herdsmen envied Abram's herdsmen; Abraham's son Ishmael envied his brother Isaac; Isaac's son Esau envied his brother Jacob; the sons of Jacob envied their brother Joseph. And on and on.

Then we come to the kings. The story of King Saul and David is one unceasing narrative of envy's undulations. David was not envious of Saul, which is why he related to Saul as a father (see 1 Samuel 24:11); but because of his insecurities, Saul was never able to be the spiritual father that David longed for. Instead, he saw David as a brother—a competitor for the throne. Saul's envy drove him to launch an eight-year military effort to extinguish David's life. David escaped—barely—and only because of God's intervention.

After his coronation, David was affronted by Cush, a Benjamite (Saul's tribe). Cush was Saul's cousin who enjoyed a position of prestige in Saul's ranks; when David became king, Cush lost his seniority. Filled with envy, Cush launched a smear campaign against David's character, trying to dethrone him. David hints at the nature of the accusations when he prays, "O LORD my God, if I have done this: If there is iniquity in my

> DAVID SHOWED US THAT WE MUST
> HONOR AND PREFER THOSE WHO ENVY US
> AND NEVER TAKE OUR DEFENSE INTO
> OUR OWN HANDS.

hands, if I have repaid evil to him who was at peace with me, or have plundered my enemy without cause, let the enemy pursue me and overtake me; yes, let him trample my life to the earth, and lay my honor in the dust. Selah" (Psalm 7:3-5). Verse 15 would suggest that Cush attempted a coup against David: "He made a pit and dug it out, and has fallen into the ditch which he made."

One of the greatest aspects of David's legacy to us is how he modeled a godly response every time he met up with envy. He never avenged himself on those who envied him, even when he had opportunity. He showed us that we must honor and prefer those who envy us and we must never take our defense into our own hands.

Anyone studying envy will undoubtedly be fascinated by the multiple circles of envy that surrounded David throughout his lifetime. Two of his sons were envious that God chose their brother Solomon for the throne; so both Absalom and Adonijah launched attempts to dethrone and kill their father, David. In this and many other ways, God used envy to help safeguard David in the midst of his successes, lest the tyranny of unbroken success should derail David from attaining the prize. The envy-motivated attacks against him kept him humble, broken, dependent and leaning on God—which is where he needed to stay.

Daniel was another man who, because of his successes, was surrounded by envy. The regional governors (Daniel's peers) under King Darius became envious of Daniel's influence with the king and connived a way to get Daniel thrown into the lion's den. Envy had caused them to forget that, years earlier, Daniel had been responsible for saving some of their lives! It was some years earlier that Nebuchadnezzar had commanded the killing of the wise men in his kingdom, but Daniel averted their deaths by telling the king the nature of his dream. But that was years ago, and the memory was gone. For them, Daniel was a competitor for position. So they conspired a plan to kill Daniel. But God sovereignly intervened and delivered him from the mouths of the lions.

Envy and Jesus
Like David and Daniel, Jesus was surrounded by a constant swirl of envy. Little wonder! No one had ever been so gifted as He was; so if those who knew Jesus had a penchant for envy, there was lots of opportunity.

Jesus had to face envy from His brothers right from the start. Can you imagine having Jesus as your older brother? Imagine having an older brother who does no wrong, who excels at everything He attempts, who has the right response in every situation, who is incredibly brilliant and exceptionally talented and has an utterly compelling connection with God! For those who have an older brother, perhaps you can relate to that a little bit.

I have just one brother, and he's older than me. All my growing-up years, I followed my brother Sheldon's footsteps. Every class I entered the teachers said things like, "Oh. You're *Sheldon's* brother." Sheldon was smarter than me, taller than me, stronger than me, a better musician than me. I know what it's like to follow behind a brother who is more gifted than you are. And yet I can't even *imagine* what it would be like to have Jesus as an older brother!

WHAT KIND OF TRANSITION WOULD A PERSON HAVE TO MAKE IN HIS MENTAL FRAMEWORK TO CONCLUDE THAT HIS OLDER BROTHER IS THE CREATOR OF THE UNIVERSE?

Jesus had four brothers (see Matthew 13:55) who couldn't bring themselves to believe in Him throughout His ministry. It wasn't until after His death and resurrection that they truly believed. What kind of transition would a person have to make in his mental framework to conclude that his older brother is the Creator of the universe? The transition was so huge that his brothers almost didn't make it. Jesus, in His mercy, helped them by appearing personally after His resurrection to the half-brother who was closest in age to Him (see 1 Corinthians 15:7).

Guess who wrote these words: "For where envy and self-seeking exist, confusion and every evil thing are there." Jesus' brother! James was Jesus' younger brother (the verse above is from James 3:16). I can hear James saying, "Guys, envy almost ate me alive! Envy was such a huge issue in my heart, it almost cost me my salvation." James was able to address the topic of envy from the authority of personal experience.

It wasn't only His brothers who envied Jesus. The religious leaders of His day envied Him intensely because they viewed Him as a competitor in their sphere. Jesus' public ministry was a constant dance of His regulating the temperature of envy in the hearts of the religious leaders. If their envy got too hot too soon, they would crucify Him prematurely. So to defuse the intensity of their envy, He would remove Himself to forsaken wilderness areas. When Jesus stepped into Jerusalem, the envy would sky-rocket at an alarming rate; so He strategically withdrew lest their envy reach the murderous stage ahead of time. For three years He regulated their envy with the skill of an artisan until the time came when it should spill over into murder.

Here is one encounter with a religious leader that is unique-ly intriguing.

> Now He was teaching in one of the synagogues on the Sabbath. And behold, there was a woman who had a spirit of infirmity eighteen years, and was bent over and could in no way raise herself up. But when Jesus saw her, He called her to Him and said to her, "Woman, you are loosed from your infirmity." And He laid His hands on her, and immediately she was made straight, and glori-fied God. But the ruler of the synagogue answered with indignation, because Jesus had healed on the Sabbath; and he said to the crowd, "There are six days on which men ought to work; therefore come and be healed on them, and not on the Sabbath day." The Lord then answered him and said, "Hypocrite! Does not each one of you on the Sabbath loose his ox or donkey from the stall, and lead it away to water it? So ought not this woman, being a daughter of Abraham, whom Satan has

bound—think of it—for eighteen years, be loosed from this bond on the Sabbath?" And when He said these things, all His adversaries were put to shame; and all the multitude rejoiced for all the glorious things that were done by Him (Luke 13:10-17).

When the synagogue ruler responded to the woman's healing with indignation, Jesus couldn't very well say, "You're just envious!" But Jesus' charge of "Hypocrite!" was an effort to show the man that he was being motivated by something other than what he was claiming. The ruler was claiming to be motivated by zeal for the Sabbath; but Jesus argued that he was showing more compassion for cattle than for people, and thus the real issue wasn't the Sabbath. His indignation was not that the Sabbath was being violated but that Jesus was demonstrating a power and authority on his home turf that he himself didn't possess. Jesus held the attention of the masses with a commanding grip that the synagogue ruler himself craved. The issue was envy.

Envy Is a Hider
The synagogue ruler veiled his envy under the guise of zeal for the Sabbath. This illustrates one of envy's common characteristics: *Envy is always a hider*. It clothes itself in the cloak of a noble passion. Envy never wants to be discovered, so it generates a noble zeal that deflects all eyes onto a secondary issue (such as the Sabbath).

The same thing happened with Joshua and Moses. Moses had called 70 elders to the tabernacle for an elder-ordaining service, but two of the appointed elders didn't come to the meeting for some reason. When the Spirit fell upon the elders, He also fell upon the two absentees who were back in the camp, and they prophesied like the other 68. A cloak of zeal came upon Joshua when he heard the two absentees were also prophesying, because he didn't think it was right that those who didn't value the meeting enough to be there were getting the same blessing. So he exclaimed, "Moses my lord, forbid them!" (Numbers 11:28). Moses' response was classic: "Are you zealous for my sake? Oh, that all the LORD'S people were prophets and that the LORD would put His Spirit upon them!" (Numbers 11:29). Joshua cloaked his envy in an appearance of holy zeal, but Moses' response showed the heart of a true father.

The chief priests' envy of Jesus finally drove them to murder Him. They didn't perceive that they were motivated by envy, however. The religious leaders were convinced they were crucifying Jesus out of justifiable and pure motives. But even an uncircumcised Gentile ruler had more discernment! It took Pilate hardly more than a moment to realize that the hatred of the Jewish leaders was fueled by envy (see Matthew 27:18; Mark 15:10).

This illustrates the incredible power of envy to deceive us to the true nature of our heart motivations. It also shows us that you don't have to be a spiritual giant to discern envy. An ungodly governor was able to recognize it instantly. When Pilate saw that he was dealing with the volatile passions of envy, he tried to help the chief priests find perspective by suggesting that Jesus be released, while Barabbas (a rebel and murderer) be prosecuted. But the chief priests were so livid with envy that they called for the release of Barabbas and the crucifixion of Jesus. At that moment, Pilate knew that he was dealing with emotions that would not accept rational argumentation. The mob was out of control. The chief priests had literally become *insane* from envy. They wanted to restore a murderer to their city streets so that they might crucify Jesus. Envy had the chief priests campaigning for brutality and murder. The story illustrates the horrific power of envy to drive men to insanely ludicrous lengths.

Let's look at just one more reading about Jesus and envy:

Then Jesus said to them, "Most assuredly, I say to you, unless you eat the flesh of the Son of Man and drink His blood, you have no life in you. Whoever eats My flesh and drinks My blood has eternal life, and I will raise him up at the last day." Therefore many of His disciples, when they heard this, said, "This is a hard saying; who can understand it?" When Jesus knew in Himself that His disciples complained about this, He said to them, "Does this offend you? What then if you should see the Son of Man ascend where He was before?" (John 6:53-54,60-62).

Jesus knew that nothing will reveal the true nature of a relationship faster than promotion. If they stumble at His giving His body and blood for them, what will they do when He is promoted to the throne of the universe? If envy had any place in their heart, Jesus knew His ascension and glorification would offend them. This principle is true in all human relationships: When someone next to you is promoted, you suddenly discover

PROMOTION tests the authenticity of Love.

the true nature of your friendship. Are you jealous or offended? Or do you swell with joy? When her son is promoted, a mother glows with pride—because a mother's love is genuine. Promotion tests the authenticity of love. When a coworker is promoted over you, your loyalty to the friendship is tested and revealed. When a brother or sister in Christ is promoted in ministry over you, will envy fill your heart or will your love be proven true?

Would John the Baptist Be Envious?

John the Baptist prepared the way for Christ and was looking passionately for His appearance. But when Christ came, perhaps the greatest test of John's loyalty would be proven by the "envy test." When the crowds would begin to leave John's meetings and gather instead at Jesus' meetings, how would John respond? The answer is given most eloquently from his own mouth.

> And they came to John and said to him, "Rabbi, He who was with you beyond the Jordan, to whom you have testified—behold, He is baptizing, and all are coming to Him!" John answered and said, "A man can receive nothing unless it has been given to him from heaven. You yourselves bear me witness, that I said, 'I am not the Christ,' but, 'I have been sent before Him.' He who has the bride is the bridegroom; but the friend of the bridegroom, who stands and hears him, rejoices greatly because of the bridegroom's voice. Therefore this joy of mine is fulfilled. He must increase, but I must decrease" (John 3:26-30).

John's disciples were alarmed by the signs of their fading ministry momentum. For the first time in their master's ministry the attendance was dropping off. John was losing popularity and Jesus was gaining it. Shouldn't John be alarmed as well? (They pretended to be zealous for John's ministry, but in fact they were envious of Jesus' ministry.)

But John would not share in their envy. He called himself "the friend of the bridegroom," and he proved his friendship by being true to Jesus, even when his ministry began to decrease. He had been standing and waiting to hear the Bridegroom's voice, and now that he heard it, John didn't simply resign himself passively to a decreasing ministry. Rather, he *rejoiced* that the Bridegroom had come and was increasing in the eyes of the bride.

John was basically saying, "My meetings are losing momentum, and I'm *thrilled* about it!" He was a true friend of the Bridegroom, for his duty was to prepare the bride for the Bridegroom. His highest dreams were fulfilled when the bride transferred her attentions from him to the Bridegroom of her affections. Envy found no place in John's heart because he himself burned with holy, passionate fire before the lover of his soul. His love was true.

DIFFERING LEVELS OF REWARD

In this chapter we've looked at envy as the dynamic that happens between brothers and between sisters as well. It rises typically among peers who function in the same general spheres of influence. Jesus told a parable that illustrates this dynamic in a compelling way.

In the parable of Matthew 20:1-16, Jesus told of a landowner who hired men to work a full 12-hour day for the wage of a denarius. Later in the day, he went out and hired another group who worked for nine hours, then another group that worked for six hours, another that worked for three hours, and, finally, another group that worked for only one hour. And yet, at the end of the day, he paid a denarius to all the laborers, regardless of how long they had worked.

When they were all paid the same wage, the men who had worked the longest complained to the employer. By paying them all equally, they argued, the landowner was giving preferential treatment to those who had worked fewer hours. Those who had labored intensely were envious of those who had worked but an hour. The fact that the landowner did not treat all his employees equally generated envy in the ranks.

Jesus used the parable to illustrate how envy surfaces when God gives varying giftings to brothers of equal standing. The truth is that God does not reward all His sons and daughters equally, at least on the surface of things. It's when we think God isn't being fair with us that envy has opportunity to find its foothold.

Here's a scenario that will become even more commonplace as Christ's return approaches. Let's suppose that you've been laboring in the Kingdom for many years; you've borne the heat of the harvest; you've labored in intercession; you've been faithful through the years. Then, as God pours out His Spirit in the last of the last days—BOOM—God suddenly brings some junkie off the streets, cleans him up and gives him a greater ministry than yours. It would appear that he gets a whole lot more from God than you ever got, with a lot less effort. And what happens in your heart? Envy! Even though you understand that God will be accelerating the preparation process in the last days, it's still very challenging to "the flesh" when you see another entering into the things for which you have labored (see John 4:38).

Jesus said, in the parable, that those who labored longest in the vineyard "complained against the landowner" (Matthew 20:11), identifying that the object of envy's complaint is actually God Himself. Envy is upset that God has been kind and generous to another brother. But our God is a good God who sometimes rewards His servants on criteria other than how diligently they have labored for Him.

The landowner (who represents God in the parable) asked those who were envious, "Or is your eye evil because I am good?" (Matthew 20:15). Envy had so filled their hearts and aroused their emotions that it was shooting out of their eyes, giving them an evil eye. An evil eye is the darkness that clouds and inflames the eye when it looks at another brother and desires what that brother has been given.

I wonder if Jesus had Proverbs 23:6 in mind when He spoke of the evil eye. The *New King James Version* uses the word "miser" in that proverb, but a literal reading is "one who has an evil eye." So an evil eye has to do with being miserly or greedy, while a good eye has to do with generosity. An evil eye does not wish generous blessings upon another. When envy darkens the eye, the spiritual ramifications are astonishing. When our eye is darkened through envy and greed, our *whole body* becomes full of darkness (see Matthew 6:23)! Therefore, the overcoming of envy in our hearts becomes all the more imperative.

God allows each of our hearts to be tested by the exact same dynamic.

The laborers in Jesus' parable struggled with envy because they all worked in the same vineyard. If they had worked in various communities, it would have been totally different. But put them all in the same vineyard and the fomenting of envy is almost inevitable.

God allows each of our hearts to be tested by the exact same dynamic. He puts us in a community or region where other servants are called of God to work in precisely the same vineyard. He places us beside other brothers or sisters who are also laboring fervently, and then He causes some to be more fruitful than others in the harvest.

What will you do when someone else's cell group grows and multiplies much more rapidly than yours? How will you feel when another church grows faster than your church, especially when that growth happens in part because of families that leave your church in favor of that other church? How will you respond when another singer on your worship team is chosen to be given a microphone rather than you? What will be the look in your eye when your sister's ministry increases while yours diminishes?

To hide our envy behind another seemingly noble motivation is deadly, both to us and to the advance of God's kingdom. Where envy remains hidden and unresolved, God's purposes are thwarted and hindered.

To confess envy and deal with its tentacles is one of the most powerful things we can do to promote the cause of Christ. Where brothers and sisters are willing to face the issues honestly, a highway is prepared for the ushering in of God's visitation in power and glory.

The process may be painful, but let's choose right now that we're going to embrace the Holy Spirit's dealings and find our way to victory over envy—so that the fame of our God might spread unhindered in all the earth!

Chapter 4

The Great Talent Showdown

tHE SINGLE MOST COMPELLING PASSAGE IN THE BIBLE RELATED TO THE SUBJECT OF THIS BOOK is found in one of Jesus' most colorful parables and is one He saved to share until the very end of His earthly ministry.

In the parable (see Matthew 25:14-30), Jesus told the story of a man who gave his goods to his servants, expecting them to improve on his investment in them by means of trading, and then he went on a journey. One servant received 5 talents of money, another received 2, and another received 1 (each according to his own ability). The first two servants doubled their master's resources over time, but the third servant buried his 1 talent in the ground.

When the master returned and saw how the first two had multiplied their talents, he said to them, "Well done, good and faithful servant; you were faithful over a few things, I will make you ruler over many things" (Matthew 25:21,23). The third servant, however, who buried his 1 talent in fear, was judged severely by the master and cast into outer darkness.

The master in the parable represents God; the servants represent God's servants whom He has gifted at differing levels of ability; and the talents of money in the parable represent the giftings, abilities and resources that God gives to His servants, expecting them to multiply and maximize those resources for the furtherance of His kingdom.

This parable relates to the different levels of giftedness with which God gifts all believers. To some He has given 1 talent; others have received 2; and still others have been given 5. In actuality, our degree of giftedness does not fall into one of three slots but rather somewhere along a vast continuum that Jesus represented by the numbers 1 and 5.

God gifts us in a wide variety of spheres, but the ministry arena where giftedness is perhaps most clearly measurable is that of music and worship. When it comes to the ministry of music, one's level of gifting is so easily measurable that you can almost put a numerical value on it. "Oh yes, she's a 3.7 when it comes to singing." "Put him on the piano, and you're listening to about a 4.5 on the gifting scale." Musical giftings are so clearly measurable that a capable minister of music can take everyone in the music department and list them by name according to degree of giftedness—from least gifted to most gifted.

Therefore, since musical giftings are so clearly measurable, I am choosing to illustrate the principles of this parable by pointing to the ministry of worship in the local church. I will leave it to the reader to make the application of these principles to other areas of ministry, such as teaching, preaching, counseling, administrating and serving.

You will notice, first of all, that Jesus said the man gave talents to each "according to his own ability" (Matthew 25:15). The Lord knows the strength of our frame and He gifts us in accordance with how much we can handle. It might be tempting to look at someone with more gifts than you and envy what they have; but the truth is that if you had their level of gifting, you would probably suffer burnout! Your frame wasn't built to handle the level of responsibility those additional giftings carry. The responsibility of stewarding that greater talent would break you. God knows you best, and He gives to you according to your strength. He loves you exactly the way you are because He has made you precisely the way He wants you to be. He loves it when you are simply you. And He won't give you more than you can effectively steward. So let's be thankful for the gifts we have and be grateful that God hasn't given us more than we can bear!

WHEN IT COMES TO TALENTS, YOU GET WHAT YOU GET.

Songwriter and worship leader David Baroni has said that envy insults God—as though by giving all that He did to my brother, He didn't have enough left over to give me my rightful portion. But with God, there's plenty to go around! So if God has limited His gifts to any of us, it is so that He might not burden us with more than we can bear.

PRINCIPLES RELATED TO TALENTS

God alone gives talents. You can't work with a talent you haven't been given. When it comes to talents, you get what you get. If He doesn't give it, you don't have it. I know some people who would love to play a musical instrument, but they could practice for the next 30 years and never become a musician! No amount of practice can give you a gift that you haven't received from God.

Sometimes someone can appear to find a gift that they didn't once have. I see four things that can make this appear to happen:

1. *Maturity:* As we grow into adulthood, sometimes there are gifts that were latent within us but that came to light simply because we grew up and learned how to access them.
2. *Awakening:* Some gifts can remain latent within us until a skillful teacher comes along who knows how to unlock what has been within all along.
3. *Cultivation:* When we are faithful to cultivate and multiply our talents, sometimes it's amazing what levels of skill we can discover. I've known people whom I thought would never rise above a 1.5 gifting in a given area, but because of their determination they managed to grow their gifting beyond a point I ever thought possible, and I would view them more like a 3.5 because of it.
4. *Download:* In some instances, God will visit someone, even in their adulthood, and divinely download to them a gift they never had previously.

So these two principles remain: You can only work with what God gives you, and talents can be grown and multiplied.

When it comes to talents, God is looking for two primary qualities: *goodness* and *faithfulness.* At the end of the day, all we want to hear is "Well done, good and faithful servant." Goodness has to do with moral integrity and uprightness; faithfulness has to do with diligence, dependability, application and hard work. The wise steward will devote himself, above all, to goodness and faithfulness.

I believe one of the best ways to cultivate your musical talent is to place yourself beside someone more musical or anointed than yourself and learn at his or her side.

When my brother, Sheldon, left for college, my mom announced to me that I would now be playing piano in church. I said, "But, Mom, I don't know how to play piano." My arguments fell on deaf ears; I was playing piano in church from now on, no discussion. Back in those days, there were only two instruments in many churches: an organ and a piano. Mom played organ, and now I was to play piano.

The first Sunday was a *disaster* (I was 14 years old at the time). I was so embarrassed that I spent the entire next week trying to bone up my skills for next Sunday's fiasco. Mom would push the organ pedal to the floor, effectively drowning over my ineptitude, and she plowed every song through to the finish. I played catch-up the whole way. As the weeks turned to months, I found myself following closer and closer behind. In time, the son was able to keep up with the mother—and in some respects even bypass her. I literally learned to play piano in church! And so I learned this valuable principle regarding talents: Stand at the side of someone who is more skilled than you, and run until you catch up.

Author and teacher Mike Bickle has offered the intriguing perspective that with the word "talents" Jesus was referring to *public* giftings. In other words, the thing that distinguishes a 4-talent person from a 3-talent person is that the 4-talent person's gifting will naturally find a more visible expression publicly among people. The greater the gifting, the more naturally that person's gift will move him or her toward a more prominent public platform. Solomon enunciated this principle when he wrote, "Do you see a man who excels in his work? He will stand before kings; He will not stand before unknown men" (Proverbs 22:29). An example can be seen in David's tabernacle in the person of Chenaniah, who rose to the prominent place of being the chief instructor of the singers "because he was skillful" (1 Chronicles 15:22). Those who are faithful to cultivate their talents and become skillful in their arena will naturally rise to and be entrusted with corresponding spheres of leadership. It's right that the more skillful and more anointed be given leadership roles in our worship ministries.

Distribution of Talents

It appears that God is totally random in the way He gives gifts to men. He doesn't give more to certain ones because they are beautiful or tall or have dark hair or are smart or have winsome personalities. The distribution of talents seemingly has no noticeable pattern to it. Why does God give 1 talent to this one and 2 talents to that one? No apparent reason. He just does. Don't ask why; you'll never get an answer. He rises up in the authority of His sovereignty and just decides arbitrarily what He will give each one. Your level of talentedness has nothing to do with His love for you. Whether He gives you 1, 2 or 5 talents, He loves you just as much as anyone else on the planet.

God gives 1 talent to this one, 2 talents to that one, 5 talents to another—and then puts them all on the same worship team and says, "Work it out." Talk about a recipe for catastrophe! Worship ministries are notorious among pastors for being one of the greatest problem areas in local church ministry. Why is that? One reason would doubtless be the fact that Satan resists the tremendous potential of worship ministries. But there's another problem, and its origins are not demonic but fleshly. I'm referring to the envy that rises up in worship teams comprised of members with differing levels of gifting. Consider again what James said about that: "For where envy and self-seeking exist, confusion and every evil thing are there" (James 3:16). When envy is allowed to exist unchecked in our worship ministries, they become haunts for "every evil thing." Nothing could be more essential than that we bring these issues into the light and call one another to repentance.

When you put people with different gift levels side by side, you're asking for problems. This terrain that we call worship team ministry is strewn with land mines. But God has a purpose for distributing multiple levels of gifting throughout the body of Christ, and I want us to explore that purpose.

THE PROBLEM OF CHURCH GROWTH

Here's how this dynamic of varying degrees of talents, working side by side, actually plays out. A new church has just started up and there are about 30 people coming to this young church. When you first plant a church, you're thankful for every 1-talent person that comes along. The guy knows one song on the banjo? He's on the worship team! This sister plays Autoharp? She's on the worship team! Frank can play guitar in the keys of G and D? Frank is now the chief musician!

Then one Sunday you walk into that church with your 2 talents. You look at that 1-talent worship ministry and think to yourself, *I have come for such a time as this.* You inform the pastor of your giftedness and your willingness to serve. The pastor looks at your 2 talents and his eyes light up. You are an answer to prayer! He wastes little time in giving you the worship ministry. In no time you have that ministry functioning in a whole new dimension. The worship in the house takes off, the spirit of praise in the congregation multiplies, the presence of God is richer than ever, and people are increasingly attracted to the atmosphere of worship. The church grows quickly from 30 to 75 and then to 130. You are the savior of the worship ministry. Everyone in the church loves you and continues to thank God repeatedly for the day He sent you to their church.

Then one Sunday morning it happens. In the back door comes . . . 5 talents! You're thinking to yourself, *Go back to the pit from which thou didst crawl!* You are shocked at the host of emotions that rise up within you as you stare at this 5-talent wonder. You know that if that woman with the 5 talents joins the worship ministry, her giftings will naturally make a way for herself, she will eventually be placed in charge of the worship ministry, and she will become the new savior of the worship team. You will be forgotten in the shadow of her exceptional giftings and wonderful spirit.

BUT THEN WHEN THE 2-TALENT PERSON LOOKS at THE 5-TALENT PERSON, HE THINKS, "LET ME CLAW YOUR EYES OUT."

I'm describing the dynamics of Ecclesiastes 4:4: "Again, I saw that for all toil and every skillful work a man is envied by his neighbor. This also is vanity and grasping for the wind." What does the 5-talent person get for all his labors in cultivating his gifting? Envy.

When the 2-talent person looks at the 1-talent person he thinks, *Move over. I'm here now. Things are going to be a little different around here.* But then when the 2-talent person looks at the 5-talent person, he thinks, *Let me claw your eyes out. Don't stay here. Don't make this your home church. Go someplace else.* The issue is envy, and it eventually surfaces in virtually every worship ministry on the face of the globe.

These dynamics are part of the growing pains of burgeoning churches. As a church grows, the level of giftedness within the various ministries of that church must grow with the corporate body. For a church of 900 people to keep growing, they will need a level of talentedness in their worship ministry that a church of 100 doesn't need. If the level of excellence in the worship ministry (and other ministries) doesn't grow with the church, the growth of the church will level off and will plateau according to the level of giftedness among its leaders. Sometimes pastors are faced with painful decisions. *Do I keep this 3-talent person over our worship ministry and keep everyone happy, or do I give the worship ministry to this 4-talent person so that we can continue to grow? But if I do that, I know some people will be offended.* Pastoring these transitions is painfully delicate.

WALKING TOGETHER

I've said that the 2-talent person looks at the 1-talent person and responds with a little bit of arrogance; and then the 2-talent person looks at the 5-talent person and responds in envy. But the 1-talent person? His or her tendency, according to Jesus, is to bury. As the excellence of the worship ministry grows, the 1-talent person says, "I quit. I'm resigning from the worship ministry.

the 5-talent person wants to get rid of the dead weight and really take off.

You guys are beyond me now. I'm too smart to stand on the platform next to all that talent. No, I'm out of here." So the 1-talent person buries the 1 talent they have.

And the 5-talent person? His tendency is to say, "Couldn't we lighten this ship a little? If we could just throw overboard some of this unnecessary tackle, we could really set the sail and make some headway!" The 5-talent person wants to get rid of the dead weight and really take off.

Jesus' parable has this to say to the 5-talent person: Slow down and bring the others with you. Your job is to teach, to instruct, to mentor, to equip, to impart to those who have lesser giftings than you. If you will be willing to slow down and bring everyone with you, you will fulfill your role in the worship ministry. You will become one who makes disciples of others.

Most of us tend to fall in the 2-talent category. We're not as gifted as some, but we're more gifted than others. It's a healthy wake-up call to realize this simple truth: There's always somebody more talented than you. We may as well get used to it. So most of us would place ourselves in this middle category. The force of the parable to us is this: Don't allow envy to rob you of your inheritance in Christ. Celebrate the successes of your 5-talent brothers. Join them in the battle; let's all go together. And be grateful that in this middle category you can serve as the mainstay and support of the worship ministry.

the Last days' battle will be won by a host of 1-talent warriors who will give their all for the sake of the King.

And what does the parable say to the 1-talent folks? Dig up your 1 talent! You simply are not permitted the luxury of keeping it buried. Go ahead: dig it up, brush it off, clean it up, and surrender it to the Master's use. I believe there is an army that will arise on the earth in the last days that will confound the powers of darkness. They will ask, "Where did this army come from?" The answer will be, "This is the army of 1-talent saints who chose to dig up their talent, clean it off and deploy it for the sake of the

Kingdom." The last days' battle will be won by a host of 1-talent warriors who will give their all for the sake of the King.

The great challenge to worship ministries today is to walk together—all the 5- and the 2- and the 1-talents—and to covenant together so that the glory of God might be revealed on Earth. Envy would seek to rob us of this thrilling adventure, but we will not submit to it for a moment. We have been made aware of the enemy's schemes. We will crucify the flesh; we will face up to the issues of our hearts and overcome in the power of the Spirit.

RELEASING THE ENTIRE BODY TO FUNCTION TOGETHER

One of the greatest leadership challenges in the church is to provide an atmosphere where the 5-talent musicians are eager to be on the team but where the 1-talent people also are warmly embraced and given a place of meaningful participation in the work of the ministry. How do we release 5-talent, 2-talent and 1-talent people all at the same time? If we are to equip all the saints for the work of ministry (see Ephesians 4:12), then we must answer this question intentionally. Although we are illustrating these dynamics by referring specifically to the ministry of worship in the local church, the talents challenge exists in virtually all areas of church ministry. It will be up to the reader to apply these principles to other venues of ministry.

A personal friend, whom I would classify as a 5-talent musician and who also has the heart of a worshiper, said to me, "I desire to be on a team that strives for excellence." This is a common sentiment among the more talented. Another friend told me he finds it very fulfilling to minister on a team with other 5-talent musicians. And yet he added, "Once upon a time I was given a chance to play and learn when I did not have the confidence that I do now." Even the 5-talent musicians have to start somewhere!

Our varying levels of giftedness set up winds of relational conflict that cannot be avoided but must be met head-on. Ministries that focus on equipping the 1-talent saints often move so slowly that the 5-talent saints don't want to be a part. The pace is simply too boring for them. Ministries that focus on releasing the 5-talent saints, however, tend to leave the 1-talent folks feeling ostracized, overshadowed, preempted and not needed. They simply can't keep up.

One church endeavored to solve this problem by forming three worship teams that functioned at three different levels of giftedness. The team with the best musicians was given more complex music that kept them from getting bored and challenged them to keep working hard. The second team was still quite good musically, but it was larger in size and was broadened to include a choir of singers. This group could flow spontaneously but still needed a lot of rehearsal. The third team was comprised of new musicians and served as the entry point to the worship ministry. Everyone started on this team and then moved up to other teams as their giftings and spirit became known. This team's music was kept simple, and they rarely moved beyond their preparation. The three teams were rotated regularly so that everyone had opportunity for expression. Unity between the three teams was guarded by having times of fellowship and sharing together.

Another church's approach was to establish a primary worship team that had the best musicians on it and which ministered most Sundays. A second worship team served as a backup to the first team, to serve when the primary worship leader was out of town. They did not rotate teams, although members from the second team were often called upon as substitutes when a member of the first team was absent. The second team served as a training ground for those with various levels of giftings. From that second team folks were sent out to function in a variety of other ministries in the church, such as home groups or the children's ministry or the youth group or the café outreach.

The International House of Prayer (IHOP) of Kansas City is discovering a fascinating solution to this challenge of mobilizing all levels of gifting. By establishing a 24/7 format of nonstop worship and prayer, there was the immediate demand for worship team members to serve round the clock. The demand made room for a wide variety of giftings and gifting levels. The 24/7 worship format also has had the delightful effect of raising the level of musicianship in the house of the Lord at an accelerated pace. It has become a safe context for worshipers to multiply their talents.[1]

The common witness of leaders is that it *is* possible to formulate a ministry that enlists all levels of giftings. One of the keys is in emphasizing a New Testament model of ministry. Those who are willing and zealous to grow in their talents and inner spirit should be granted a place in the midst. If we make excellence our goal, then many will be ostracized; but when we emphasize calling and heart motivation, there's room for all who are called. It's amazing to watch someone with lesser giftings have a far greater ministry impact than might have been expected because he has a burning passion for Jesus that ignites the hearts of others.

The wise pastor will find ways for the 5-talent musicians to soar. While they must train up the others, they also must have an outlet for their creative abilities. When 5-talent people are given the freedom to stretch their wings, they will create a wind-tunnel effect—the momentum of their forward movement will make a way for others to follow. The bottom line is that we must be committed to walking out together the difficult dynamics that emerge because of our various levels of giftedness. The Scriptures tell us that "love does not envy" (1 Corinthians 13:4), so when we truly walk in love with each other, we will do violence to the carnal passions aroused by envy.

Thorn in the Flesh

The worship ministry is one of the most powerful ministries in the church. When the presence of God descends upon the anointed Levites as they stand and minister to the Lord, the chain reactions that can begin to happen in the Spirit are absolutely powerful and potentially intoxicating to those God uses in this way. If the worship ministry had nothing to keep it in balance, it could easily become ego-centered and ambition driven.

> the fact that we have to work
> with each other with our differing
> talents keeps us humble, dependent
> and leaning on God.

But God has given the worship ministry a balancing stick. I call it their thorn in the flesh. It's the disparity of talents on the team. God has sovereignly and purposefully built this tension into our systems of ministry so that we are forced to face the attitudes of our hearts with honesty. Our kindness is tested; our patience is tested; our faithfulness is tested; our love is tested. The fact that we have to work with each other with our differing talents keeps us humble, dependent and leaning on God. And *that's* why He gave the multiplicity of talents. It's actually our safety and salvation. Without it, we wouldn't even be able to live with psalmists!

The call of Scripture to prefer (or honor) one another challenges everybody. When the 1-talent saints prefer the 5-talent saints by giving them place to soar, the 5-talent people will show up the 1-talent people for how untalented they really are. This will test the hearts of the 1-talent people intensely. Will they accuse the 5-talent people of being performance oriented and operating in the strength of the flesh?

On the other hand, when the 5-talent people prefer the 1-talent people by stepping back and giving them a platform for expression, it will test the hearts of the 5-talent people as they take a secondary role, all the while knowing they could do it better themselves. Will they accuse the 1-talent people of being envious?

What the Holy Spirit is testing in all of our hearts is this: Are we preferring one another in love?

The Star on the Team
One time when I took my son Michael to one of his basketball games, his team played a team that had a star player on it. When this particular boy was on the court, their team chalked up all kinds of points. When he sat on the bench, my son's team would stage a comeback. But the comeback wouldn't last long enough, because then the star would get back on the court and their team would take off again.

Have you ever played on a team where you spent a lot of time sitting on the bench and watching your team's star player start every game, get the most playing time of anybody and then also finish the game? You have a choice in that position; either you can be envious or you can decide to be glad that he or she is on your team.

I'm about to confess one of the ugly instances of envy in my life. I know that my friends who read this will use it against me for the rest of my life (in good humor of course), but I guess that's the point. If I'll confess my stinking envy and allow others to tease me about it, maybe I'll gain more grace to overcome. So here goes. I was flipping through a Christian magazine one day and kept coming across one name. The name was advertised for this event, for that cruise, for having written this book, and so on. Then on the best-seller list, his name was right there at the top. The name was Max Lucado. Now, I've never met Max Lucado, nor have I ever been in the same room with him. I could pass him on the street and never know it was him. So I stopped and thought to myself, *Why does this guy bug me? I've never met the man, and he bugs me.* And just that quickly the Holy Spirit whispered in my heart, "Envy." Suddenly I saw it—I was envious of Max Lucado! And why? Because it was *his* book that was the number one best-seller and not mine!

Well, I repented immediately, of course. But the issue wasn't Max Lucado; the issue was in my heart. Then I discovered the following month, when reading the magazine, that I had new opportunities for envy because it was *somebody else* who was the best-selling author that month. I've come to realize there will always be somebody more gifted than me. So I had better get used to it and deal with the issues.

Several times the Lord has had to say to me, in regard to others who are more talented or anointed than me, "Why can't you rejoice that they're on your team?" So by His grace, that is what I have purposed I will do.

It's easy for 5-talent people to fall into the trap of relying upon their natural strengths. Sometimes they can begin to feel

Jesus never made room for others by backing off from His own calling.

self-sufficient, as though they don't need others. And sometimes they can plow right over people in their pursuit of their goals. If you're a 5-talent person with the heart of David, perhaps God will keep you in check by giving you a Saul. While you're playing your harp skillfully to the Lord, Saul will try to drive a javelin through your heart. Saul was actually God's gift to David, to keep him humble in the midst of his anointing.

I've watched some of the most talented musicians function in some of the least anointing, because they can easily get caught up in focusing on musical proficiency at the expense of going deep in God. They've got an impressive flame but not much oil. Many of the people are fooled, but those who have discernment

EARLY ON, THE TWELVE HAD TO MAKE A CHOICE: EITHER GET INTIMIDATED BY THIS MAN OR GET FASCINATED BY HIM.

know the difference. God has ways of teaching the 5-talent people that they are absolutely nothing apart from His grace and anointing. Learning that lesson is sometimes painful.

LEARNING FROM JESUS

I don't think anyone would argue that Jesus was a 5-talent man. Yea, more than 5 talents! So how did Jesus interact with the various levels of talentedness among His disciples?

First of all, Jesus never stepped aside from His mandate or dumbed down for the sake of those following Him. He never said, "John, it's your turn to teach today. I'm just going to listen." And He never said, "Peter, it's your turn to heal the people today. I'm going to sit over here and watch." In other words, He never made room for others by backing off from His own calling. He put the pedal to the metal and invited His disciples to stand at His side and watch, and thus they were changed in His presence. Early on, the Twelve had to make a choice: either get intimidated by this Man or get fascinated by Him, enjoy Him and learn at His side. Even though Jesus was more gifted than they were, they purposed to turn from envy and to be exhilarated with the delight of walking in His shadow.

I see this general pattern in how Jesus raised up ministries: He taught and modeled; then He sent them out in pairs to do what He was doing, all the while continuing His own ministry. Then He listened to their report, giving them feedback and correction; and then He told them to stay at His side once again to watch and learn. So the cycle was repeated again. Eventually the time came for separation. By the time Jesus separated Himself from them, they were prepared to function on their own.

When it comes to envy, there's another important principle I've gleaned from Jesus' life. I discovered it in this passage:

> Then James and John, the sons of Zebedee, came to Him, saying, "Teacher, we want You to do for us whatever we ask." And He said to them, "What do you want Me to do for you?" They said to Him, "Grant us that we may sit, one on Your right hand and the other on Your left, in Your glory." But Jesus said to them, "You do not know what you ask. Are you able to drink the cup that I drink, and be baptized with the baptism that I am baptized with?" They said to Him, "We are able." So Jesus said to them, "You will indeed drink the cup that I drink, and with the baptism I am baptized with you will be baptized; but to sit on My right hand and on My left is not Mine to give, but it is for those for whom it is prepared." And when the ten heard it, they began to be greatly displeased with James and John. But Jesus called them to Himself and said to them, "You know that those who are considered rulers over the Gentiles lord it over them, and their great ones exercise authority over them. Yet it shall not be so among you; but whoever desires to become

great among you shall be your servant. And whoever of you desires to be first shall be slave of all. For even the Son of Man did not come to be served, but to serve, and to give His life a ransom for many" (Mark 10:35-45).

James and John wanted a place of special privilege at Jesus' throne. When the other 10 disciples heard of their request, they were "greatly displeased." Why? Because of envy. When Jesus realized that their request had surfaced all this envy, Jesus called the whole group of disciples to Himself and took the matter in hand.

How did Jesus deal with their envy? I would have expected Him to get out a sledgehammer and deal violently with such a dark, slimy, ugly, pernicious sin. But here's the important principle: When correcting envy, Jesus did it with gentleness.

when correcting envy, Jesus did it with gentleness.

Can you see the gentleness of His response? This teaches me volumes. This tells me that when I see envy in our worship ministry (or any other church ministry), I should deal with it promptly and diligently—but *gently*. When correcting envy, we must call each other in gentleness to the crucified life. Let us humble ourselves and serve one another. Let us stay soft of heart and keep crying out for mercy. Pride and ambition will bow in the presence of this kind of gentle correction.

TO TALENTS AND BEYOND

I give thanks to God for the talents He gives us; but this chapter wouldn't be complete if I didn't add this thought: There is another dimension beyond talents. There is a dimension of

ministry in God's grace whereby our ministry effectiveness tran-
scends our degree of talents. This is good news indeed! Let me
point you to it.

Let's start with 5-talent Joseph. Joseph was the multitalented
guy who could do everything. Potiphar gave the full administra-
tion of his household to Joseph's oversight because everything
Joseph touched was blessed of God. He impressed everybody
with his ability to juggle multiple tasks with grace and aptitude.
With his 5 talents, Joseph was able to run an entire household
(see Genesis 39).

THERE IS A DIMENSION of MINISTRY IN GOD'S GRACE WHEREBY OUR MINISTRY effectiveness TRANSCENDS OUR DEGREE of taLENTS.

But God had so much more than just a household for
Joseph: He had a *nation* for Joseph to administrate. And yet, God
knew that if Joseph was going to be effective in leading a nation,
he would have to find a reservoir within himself that was deeper
than his natural talents. To help Joseph find that other dimension, God put him in prison. Prison is the place where all the
strengths and giftings you've cultivated are now rendered use-
less. In the lonely confinement of his dank Egyptian dungeon,
I can imagine Joseph crying out to God with an unparalleled
desperation: "God, why have You allowed this? Why have Your
promises not worked in my life? I have only obeyed and loved
You; and now here I am, a prisoner in Egypt, and I've done nothing to deserve it. God, where are You? If You don't talk to me, I'm
going to *die* in this prison!"

The desperation pushed Joseph to press into the Spirit of
God in a way like he had never done in all his life. He used the

abundance of boredom as an opportunity to seek the Spirit of God with unprecedented intensity. He put roots down in God, deeper, deeper, deeper. And then one day he found the river! He found the river of abiding in the Spirit of God. He found a source in God that runs deeper than the seasons of life. He found such a source in God that, when Pharaoh had his dream, Joseph was able to draw upon that river of life and give Pharaoh the interpretation of his dream. It was Joseph's ability to access the depths of the Spirit that liberated him from his prison.

In one day Joseph went from the prison to the palace. And the issue for Joseph was this: Will you feed a household, or will you feed nations? To be a pastor to the nations, Joseph, you're going to have to find a source in God that goes way beyond your giftings. Your giftings are great, but they'll never empower you to do what God has for you. But now, because you found the river, you will become a dispenser of life to the nations of the earth.

And then there's Anna (see Luke 2:36-38). I call her 1-talent Anna. Nothing in the biblical account would suggest that Anna had any outstanding giftings or abilities. She didn't have any marketable skills, but she knew she could do one thing: she could be a wife and mother. But after seven years of marriage, God snuffed out the life of her husband. This catastrophe sent Anna reeling. "God, how could You remove the light of my eyes? How could You destroy every vision I ever had for my life? You have taken from me the one thing I could do."

In the grief of that moment, Anna had a choice. She could become bitter against God, or she could press deeper into God than ever before. Choosing the latter, Anna began to seek God with her entire being. "God, I don't know why You've devastated my life. I can't see Your goodness in my life, yet I declare that You are a good God, and I'm going to seek You until I see Your goodness. I declare You are a loving God, even though it sure doesn't feel like You love me right now; but I know You are a loving God, and I'm going to seek You until I see Your love in my life." And Anna began to press into the Spirit of God like never before.

And then one day she heard the voice. "Fasting and prayer? Night and day? Okay, Lord, if You say so." She turned the furnace up seven times hotter and began to give herself to fasting and prayer, ministering to the Lord night and day.

The months turned into years, and then the voice came again. "MESSIAH?? Oh, my Lord, Messiah!!" God had shown her that the Messiah was soon to be born and that by her intercessions Anna was fulfilling a critical role in preparing the way through prayer. With redoubled urgency she travailed in intercession for the Messiah. And then the day came when she held the answer to her prayers in her own arms! I don't think I'm stretching the story when I suggest that Anna prayed in the Messiah.

Anna is the 1-talent woman who could have become a casualty through bitterness; but because she pressed into the face of God, the Lord turned her barrenness into fruitfulness, and now she is a spiritual mother to the entire household of faith. She thought God had buried her 1 talent, when in reality God was inviting her to a dimension that superceded it.

Give thanks to God for your talents, whether they be 5, 2 or 1. And do your utmost to cultivate them faithfully to their fullest expression. But if the Lord should invite you to a higher dimension, allow Him to press you into His face with unprecedented desperation. Perhaps He would lead you to the other dimension, which is "'not by might, nor by power, but by My Spirit,' says the LORD of hosts" (Zechariah 4:6).

Note

1. See www.fotb.com for more information on the ministry of International House of Prayer (IHOP).

Chapter 5

WHY REVIVAL TARRIES

WHENEVER GOD BREAKS OUT IN REVIVAL POWER AND GLORY, there is invariably an accompanying outbreak of envy. It came against Jesus in His earthly ministry and also against the apostles as they took the gospel to the nations. It's especially fascinating to study the eruptions of envy that followed Paul in his missionary travels.

- The first eruption came on the island of Paphos, where Elymas the sorcerer withstood Paul and tried to turn the proconsul away from the faith because he envied and feared the authority on Paul's life (see Acts 13:6-8).
- At Antioch in Pisidia (see Acts 13:14-50), Paul preached the gospel in the synagogue on the Sabbath. The Jews weren't very moved, but the Gentiles begged Paul and

Barnabas to return the following Sabbath to preach again. When they did so, "almost the whole city came together to hear the word of God" (v. 44). Well, guess what *that* did! Seeing a multitude of people gathering around the apostles stirred up a cauldron of envy among the Jews. Immediately they began to contradict, blaspheme and oppose the message. So Paul and Barnabas pulled out of the synagogue and preached to the Gentiles at another location. But that didn't satisfy the envy of the Jews, who "stirred up the devout and prominent women and the chief men of the city, raised up persecution against Paul and Barnabas, and expelled them from their region" (v. 50).

- At Iconium, the Jews tried similar tactics of discrediting the gospel. But when that wasn't successful, they plotted to stone the apostles who, hearing of the plot, fled to Lystra and Derbe (see Acts 14:1-6).

- At Lystra, the gospel was having powerful effect until the envious Jews from Antioch and Iconium came to Lystra, stirred up the people against the apostles and persuaded them to stone Paul (see Acts 14:8-20). But God raised Paul up, presumably from the dead.

- At Thessalonica, when a great multitude of Gentiles believed, the Jews became envious and gathered a mob to try to kill the apostles (see Acts 17:1-10).

- In Berea, both Jews and Gentiles were coming to the Lord, and all was well until the Jews from Thessalonica heard about the revival in Berea. Filled with envy, they came to Berea and, stirring up the crowds, forced the apostles to leave town (see Acts 17:10-15).

- In Corinth, the Lord graciously kept the envious factions from boiling over. This gave Paul an exceptional door of opportunity in Corinth, where he was able to stay for 18 months of fruitful ministry. When the unbelieving Jews finally did attempt (because of envy) to take Paul to court (see Acts 18:12), the plot unraveled, and Paul was able to remain in town for "a good while" (Acts 18:18).

All these envy-motivated persecutions were the direct result of revival. When God begins to move, the enemies of the gospel (which are sometimes those in tradition-bound religious systems) will find all kinds of ways to justify their envy, and they will persecute the genuine move of the Spirit of God.

When the enemies of the gospel are envious and resistant, that is standard fare for the Kingdom. It's part of the territory, part and parcel of the persecution that Jesus promised we would have to endure. But it's not only the enemies of the gospel who

it's the envy of God's people that poses the great impediment to revival.

are envious when revival breaks out. When God visits His people, sometimes the most insidious forms of envy develop within the hearts of the very preachers of the gospel themselves. We are ready for our enemies to be resistant and envious; but we aren't ready for it to come from our friends! I am suggesting that the great problem of revival does not come from outside the church but from within the church. It's the envy of God's people that poses the great impediment to revival.

ENVY IN THE CHURCH

Herein is the great problem! Revival is not impeded so much by envy from segments of the pseudochurch (liberal/humanistic groups who have a form of godliness but deny its power). Instead, the great historic hindrance to revival is envy that springs up in the hearts of genuinely born-again, Spirit-filled, Bible-believing, blood-washed Christians who watch the revival from a distance and envy the blessing of God upon another brother's ministry.

I am not suggesting that envy is the *only* hindrance to revival (truly there are many). But if discord in the body of Christ is one of the primary hindrances to revival, what could be the foremost cause of that discord if not envy? Furthermore, the problem of envy is not primarily that of the common people in our churches but, rather, that of the leaders. If the shepherds were reconciled, the sheep would gladly fellowship. When revival comes, it's not sheep who envy what's happening but the shepherds. The brothers.

if the shepherds were reconciled, the sheep would gladly fellowship.

Literally every century of church history is laden with explosions of envy that erupted among God's people when the winds of revival touched down in specific places. I will quote from just one example. At the beginning of the twentieth century, God used the healing ministry of John G. Lake to bring many converts into the Kingdom. But where revival exists, envy is also there. The following is from a letter written by the hand of John G. Lake on December 15, 1910, during his ministry in South Africa:

> I received today mail from Los Angeles, CA, containing copies of letters written by false brethren here. These letters have been sent worldwide denouncing me as all that was wicked and unholy. I also received a most unholy

letter from one George Bowie, a man who apparently is
or was a Christian worker of some kind, but who seems
to be consumed with envy and jealousy. This is the opinion of all the American brethren with whom I am close-
ly associated who assure of their confidence. . . . I never
knew such terrific malice and envy to exist before as is
shown by Mr. Cooper, Mr. Bowie, Gillis, and others.[1]

It's safe to assume that Lake's detractors did not realize they
were motivated by envy. They were convinced, I am sure, that
their crusade against his ministry was justifiable and a noble
service to God. Such is the masquerading power of envy.

Envy killed Jesus—and it's still killing Him today.

Recently I visited Atlanta, Georgia, where there are over 60
churches each with a weekly attendance in excess of 3,000 people.
I was told that a pastor in Atlanta doesn't have a voice to the larger church of Atlanta "unless you bring at least 3,000 people to the

WHEN YOU RECEIVE a SUDDEN WINDfaLL
of BOTH HUMAN AND fiNANCIAL RESOURCES
BECAUSE of THE move of GOD, every OTHER
BROTHER IN YOUR SPHERE of
MINISTRY takes IMMEDIATE NOTICE.

table." Those who have the most human resources carry the most
clout in our church cultures. This appearance of what constitutes
power and authority is the seedbed upon which envy thrives.

When revival hits, two things typically begin to gather in
abundance: people and money. Crowds convene in unprecedented numbers, and along with the people comes a flow of giving as
the saints offer their thanksgiving to God for His blessings.
When you receive a sudden windfall of both human and financial

resources because of the move of God, every other brother in your sphere of ministry takes immediate notice. Those with noble hearts offer their blessing to the revival, but there isn't a single leader who doesn't have to wrestle with some feeling of envy when another brother is the one selected by God for revival.

A CONTEMPORARY EXAMPLE

I have visited with Joe, a personal friend, regarding a revival that happened in recent years in his city. He was there before the revival came and, although he was not personally a member of the church where the revival happened, he was able to watch from start to finish the explosive move of God in genuine revival. When the revival hit, news spread quickly among the over 400 churches in the city. Believers from a wide variety of area churches began to flock to the meetings as reports of God's activity proliferated.

Then the inevitable began to happen: People began to leave their churches and transfer to the church where the revival was happening. Almost every church in town lost someone to the revival. Pastors became upset, wounded or hurt. Many judgments were made by pastors who, according to my friend Joe, didn't attend even one meeting of the revival. Some pastors took a stand against the revival in the hope that people would stop leaving their churches. Inevitably, each pastor in town had to make his own stand regarding the revival. In most cases, that early judgment has been maintained to this day.

The pastor who was hosting the revival did his utmost to reassure his fellow pastors in the community that he and his staff were doing everything in their power to walk in integrity. They were telling people to go back to their home churches and that their tithe belonged in their home church, not the revival meetings. Pastors from other churches were welcome to follow up on any documented decisions for Christ. In short, the host pastor did his best to show that he wanted the revival to be a regional revival and not just something sponsored by a single local church. But his best efforts could not quell the envy.

The local news media took such an adversarial position toward the revival that one could almost wonder if the editorial staff were not directly influenced by the envy of the respective churches where they worshiped.

WHAT IS GOD TO DO?

God *wants* to send revival to your city! But here's the problem: No matter which church or ministry He selects to become the catalyst for that revival, the other brothers in town will struggle with envy. Some of the brothers (i.e., area pastors and leaders) will be able to overcome their envy, crucify their flesh and join in the revival with enthusiasm and energy. But many of the brothers in the region will not be able to discern and deal with their

> before sending revival,
> God has to weigh the envy
> factor in the region.

envy. They will find ways to justify their criticism of what's happening and will conclude it's not a true revival. So then what God intended as a blessing to the region becomes a cause of contention and strife.

God is caught many times between the proverbial rock and hard place. If He doesn't send revival, the kingdom of God does not penetrate society and the end-time harvest is not brought in. But if He does send revival, the eruption of envy in the church is so destructive and counterproductive to the extension of the

Kingdom that the blessing of revival turns into a curse. Because of envy, the house of blessing (revival) becomes a haunt for "every evil thing"! (James 3:16).

Before sending revival, God has to weigh the envy factor in the region. How have the brothers (leaders) of the region responded to God's dealings in their hearts in the area of envy? If they have embraced repentance, humility and brokenness over the natural tendencies of their hearts toward carnal comparisons and ambitious self-seeking, God will be able to visit that region with power and glory. But if subtle shades of competition have not been met violently with radical repentance, God must withhold revival lest the eruption of envy bring a curse that outweighs any blessing revival would bring.

One of the keys to sustaining revival in a region is unity within the church of that region. And one of the greatest hindrances to unity is envy. When leaders refuse to take their envy to the cross and leave it there, the blessing of God will eventually dissipate.

I am fascinated by a syndrome I've observed related to revival. When God touches down and visits a church with revival, people will come from other regions, other states and even other nations to bask in the flow of God's blessings. *Everybody* will come to the revival—except the brothers of the same city. Because envy is always an issue between the brothers.

The apostles faced a test, without realizing it, that was to determine whether they would be visited with revival. The test surrounded the selecting of a replacement for Judas Iscariot's office. Transitions in leadership are always very sensitive moments in the realm of envy. It came down to two names: "Joseph called Barsabas, who was surnamed Justus, and Matthias" (Acts 1:23).

Now, the selection of who would be the twelfth apostle of the Lamb was no small matter. The implications were both huge and eternal. And it was all determined by a straw vote. When Matthias was chosen by lot, that's when the great test came. Would Joseph or those who favored him become envious? Would they allow the favor bestowed on Matthias to become an occasion for dissension and contention? Thankfully, neither Joseph nor his friends gave in to envy. Instead they joined their hearts with Matthias and all the others for the greater purposes of the Kingdom. And so it was that the Scripture could testify, "When the Day of Pentecost had fully come, they were all with one accord in one place" (Acts 2:1). All with one accord! How beautiful is this unity that has not given any place to bitter envy and strife! Surely it is this kind of unity that God can honor by sending His Holy Spirit in manifest power and glory.

tHeRe is a geNeRatioN tHat wiLL DeaL witH tHe envy issue straigHt oN.

Beloved, my heart cries and yearns for true apostolic revival. Oh, to see the manifest power and glory of God in our day! It's everything I live for. How I long to see the Word preached with authority; to see the conviction of the Spirit settle upon sinful hearts; to see blind eyes opened, deaf ears unstopped, the lame walking and the dead raised; to see stadiums overflowing with seekers and stadium floors filled with penitent hearts seeking salvation; to see cities shaken for God! It's the hope that the Scriptures set before us, that God will send a Spirit-empowered revival of historic proportions to gather the great end-time harvest before the return of Christ. It's our longing, our hope, the great object of our unceasing intercessions.

But revival has one great enemy. How could there be a more potent hindrance to revival than envy?

Conversely, how could there be a greater contributor to revival than the melting of all envious divides? When the brothers of a community bring their envy into the light, confess it freely, repent of it and posture their hearts to celebrate the advance of the Kingdom no matter whom God chooses to use, they make themselves a prime target for revival.

There *is* a generation that will deal with the envy issue straight on. They will not hide from it; they will not call it something else; they will not justify it with a false zeal; they will not let shame keep them from confessing it. They will say with simple forthrightness, "I have a problem with envy. Lord Jesus, forgive me! Cleanse me. Root out the self-seeking ambition from my heart that doesn't want to celebrate my brother's successes. Give me a clean heart, I pray, O God." The generation that will walk in *this* light will be the generation that will see revival.

Will it be this generation?

And what must be done to deal with the envy of our hearts? To answer this great question we now dedicate the remainder of this book.

Note

1. *John G. Lake: The Complete Collection of His Life Teachings,* comp. Roberts Liardon (Tulsa, OK: Albury Publishing, 1999), pp. 97, 99.

CHAPTER 6

THE CROSS: DEATH OF ENVY

GOD DEALS WITH ENVY AT THE CROSS. As a work of the flesh it must be thrust through and killed. We have been crucified with Christ (see Galatians 2:20), which means we now have the power to live as though our flesh were dead. And every time the flesh attempts to resurrect itself, we once again count ourselves dead to sin and alive to God (see Romans 6:11). The Cross is the answer to every work of the flesh. When the flesh has been crucified, it is dead to sin. Therefore, every time we repent and embrace the crucified life, we "die daily" (1 Corinthians 15:31) so that sins like envy might have no dominion over us.

However, the Cross also deals with envy in another way. Jesus' cross was the implement that empowered Jesus' brothers

to overcome their envy. Up until His crucifixion, Jesus' four natural half-brothers were simply incapable of rising above their
envy and putting their faith in their older brother. His teachings,
His miracles, His lifestyle, His supernatural birth as told to them
by their mother—all were compelling, but they could never rise
above the fact that this was their *brother*. Envy was literally keeping them from eternal life (see John 7:3-8). So God's answer was
the Cross.

There is good reason to suppose that Jesus' brothers were
present at His crucifixion. (It happened during the feast of
Passover, a feast at which attendance for all Jewish males was
mandatory; and it seems highly improbable they would be in the
city but not present at the crucifixion.) When they beheld Jesus
on the cross, everything changed for them. The torment of His
suffering and the dignity with which He bore it made their mark
in their hearts. They saw a suffering that surpassed comprehension. How could they gaze upon this crucified form, which
didn't even resemble a man because of its gruesomeness (see
Isaiah 52:14), and continue to envy Him? As their envy melted at
the foot of the Cross, the sprouting seeds of faith were finally
given opportunity within their hearts to rise.

When they saw His supernatural death and resurrected
body, they believed. (We know that at least one of Jesus' brothers—James—saw Jesus in His resurrected body, according to
1 Corinthians 15:7.) The cross was the catalyst that empowered
Jesus' brothers to overcome their envy and transition over into
faith, which is why they were present in the Upper Room when
the Holy Spirit was poured out on the 120 disciples (see Acts
1:13–2:4).

The Cross dealt with the brothers' envy.

This is still how God deals with envy among the brothers. He
crucifies the brother whom He has selected for honor.

I said, "Lord, if my brother is envying me, then shouldn't *he* be the one who gets crucified since it's his problem?" The Lord says, "No, I'm going to deal with your brother's envy by crucifying *you*." This pattern is proven throughout Scripture. Let me give you some examples.

JACOB AND ESAU

Esau hated Jacob because Jacob had stolen their father's blessing. With Esau being envious to the point of murder, Jacob is sent away by his mother to find a wife in Padam Aram. When Jacob returns to Esau 20 years later, he comes with two wives, 11 sons and a multitude of livestock. But Jacob is still extremely afraid of his brother's envy, so he sends several lavish gifts of livestock to his brother, with the gifts preceding his presence.

Twenty years of separation will help dissipate envy, and lavish gifts will certainly help to win Esau's favor. But God is going to take one additional measure to be sure that Esau's envy is dealt with. God visits Jacob the night before he is to meet up with Esau and gives Jacob his own unique identification with the cross. He shrinks the muscle in Jacob's hip, causing Jacob to limp severely (see Genesis 32:22-32). I'm convinced this was an excruciating experience for Jacob, and the limp was in part because of the pain involved in walking. So when Jacob walked forward to meet his brother, Esau, he was quite the spectacle with his fresh wound from the night before. Jacob still didn't know how to adjust his body to this mark of God in his flesh, so he awkwardly limped toward his brother. The sight of this wincing, limping man was the final element in helping to quiet the envy of Esau's heart so that he could receive his brother. Envy melted into pity, and the brothers were reunited.

We think God should remove envy by dealing with the hearts of those who harbor the envy. But sometimes He deals with it by crucifying the one who is envied.

JOSEPH AND HIS BROTHERS

Joseph was his father's favorite son, which had marked him for envy from his brothers. But when he told his brothers of the dreams he had—that his brothers would bow down to him—their envy expanded exponentially. Joseph's brothers didn't realize

GOD DEALS WITH THE ENVY AMONG BROTHERS BY TURNING THE CHOSEN BROTHER INTO A SPIRITUAL FATHER.

that God's promises to Joseph were in fact intended for the benefit of *all* the brothers. They were too distracted by the fact that *they* weren't chosen to be the channel of blessing. When the opportunity came, they nearly murdered him but then sold him as a slave instead. Their hearts were so envious of Joseph that nothing in the world—or so they thought—would cause them to bow before their brother!

When Joseph was given the throne of Egypt, being second only to Pharaoh, his brothers would certainly bow before him out of fear. But Joseph's promotion in and of itself would not take care of their envy. In fact, it had the potential to only make it worse.

So what would God do to deal with the envy of Joseph's brothers? God's answer was to crucify Joseph, in a metaphorical way. In actuality, it meant 13 years of slavery and imprisonment for Joseph.

When Joseph's brothers later realized that Joseph's position was gained at such a high price, their envy was diffused and they were able to honor their brother with an open spirit. I say that based upon their response to Joseph after their father Jacob's death (see Genesis 50:15-21). Instead of distancing themselves from Joseph in envy, they "fell down before his face, and they said, 'Behold, we are your servants'" (Genesis 50:18). With envy out of the way, they were able to relate to Joseph in an honoring way.

Let me say it in another way. God deals with the envy among brothers by turning the chosen brother into a spiritual father. Joseph's crucible was intended by God, not to make him just a brother, but to make him a father. He actually became a spiritual father to his brothers. When Joseph became like a father to his brothers, the envy issue was silenced, because sons generally don't envy fathers. The crucible that dissipates the brothers' envy also promotes the chosen one to spiritual fatherhood.

JOB'S BROTHERS

We know that God had chosen Job for an unusual and most glorious revelation of the throne of God, besides the blessings of children, grandchildren and possessions. Such glorious privilege could certainly have caused Job's brothers to envy him.

We are given only one tiny peek into Job's relationship with his brothers, and it's found in their response to Job after his great trial: "Then all his brothers, all his sisters, and all those who had been his acquaintances before, came to him and ate food with him in his house; and they consoled him and comforted him for all the adversity that the LORD had brought upon him. Each one gave him a piece of silver and each a ring of gold" (Job 42:11).

Isn't it interesting that after experiencing a revelatory encounter with the glory of God and a supernatural release of divine power in healing that, instead of being envied by them, Job is actually consoled and comforted with gifts from his brothers. What could cause his brothers to relate to him in such affection, knowing that he had been chosen instead of them for spiritual privilege?

The answer, of course, is found in the Cross. God crucified Job. Well, not literally; but Job certainly shared in the sufferings of Christ by suffering according to the will of God. He lost virtually everything—his children, his possessions, his health, his friends. It was because God crushed him that Job's brothers were able to relate to him without envy.

DAVID AND HIS BROTHERS

We are told that Samuel anointed David as king of Israel "in the midst of his brothers" (1 Samuel 16:13). It's so tempting to think, *Bad move, Samuel! David doesn't have a chance now. By anointing him in the presence of his brothers, you have set him up for such "decibels" of envy that he may never be able to recover from it. Don't you think, Samuel, that it would have been wiser to anoint him privately, without his brothers knowing about it?* But God strategically purposed that David would have to deal with the envy of his brothers.

And it's not hard to see their envy. When David brings them some refreshments on the battlefield and then makes an inquiry about the Philistine giant, Goliath, David's oldest brother erupts with the venom of envy.

> Now Eliab his oldest brother heard when he spoke to the men; and Eliab's anger was aroused against David, and he said, "Why did you come down here? And with whom have you left those few sheep in the wilderness? I know your pride and the insolence of your heart, for you have come down to see the battle" (1 Samuel 17:28).

Eliab's expression of envy toward David on this occasion was only the tip of the iceberg. David's other six brothers also carried similar feelings in their hearts. The bitterness that envy had produced was very intense.

And yet it's only a few short chapters later that David's brothers actually seek David out and join up with him. "David therefore departed from there and escaped to the cave of Adullam. And when his brothers and all his father's house heard it, they went down there to him" (1 Samuel 22:1).

What would cause such a dramatic change in their hearts toward David? Well, to put it simply, it was David's crucifixion that changed things. When Saul turned on David, trying repeatedly to kill him, and then began to chase him around the countryside, David's brothers had a total change of heart. If David had ascended to the throne easily and quickly, they wouldn't have been able to handle it. But because God took him through such a circuitous, agonizing route, their envy was dissipated and they were able to join up with their brother whom God had sovereignly chosen.

The pattern in Scripture is quite stunning: God deals with the envy of the brothers by crucifying His chosen one.

THE TWO KINGDOMS

After Solomon's reign, the nation of Israel was divided into two kingdoms. The northern kingdom of Israel was eventually headquartered in the city of Samaria; the southern kingdom of Judah was based at the capital city of Jerusalem. For many generations there were two kings in Israel—one in the north and one in the south. And as a result, an ongoing rivalry existed between the two.

The northern kingdom was especially envious of the southern kingdom of Judah because, having Jerusalem within its domain, Judah possessed the Temple mount and hence the priesthood, the sacrifices, the Ark of the Covenant and the "smile" of God. The rivalry continued for generation after generation, until it was obvious that the two nations were never going to come together of their own volition.

But God needed them to come together. It was essential, in His wisdom and counsel, that the nation not be divided when His Son, the Messiah, would come to establish the kingdom of God on Earth. Something had to happen for the two to become one. What was God's solution? Well, it was a crucifixion of sorts. We refer to it as the captivity, or the exile. God's answer was to

envy is a peacetime problem.

send His people to Babylon for 70 years of captivity in a foreign land. He used Nebuchadnezzar to enforce the captivity, whose forces invaded Judah and carried the people of God off to modern-day Iraq.

Isaiah was the one who prophesied of God's purpose in using the captivity to make the two nations into one.

> Also the envy of Ephraim shall depart, and the adversaries of Judah shall be cut off; Ephraim shall not envy Judah, and Judah shall not harass Ephraim. But they shall fly down upon the shoulder of the Philistines toward the west; together they shall plunder the people of the East; they shall lay their hand on Edom and Moab; and the people of Ammon shall obey them (Isaiah 11:13-14).

The passage speaks of how the two kingdoms would "envy" and "harass" each other. The competitiveness between the tribes was powerful. But if these dynamics had still been at work among God's covenant people when Jesus had come to Earth, His ministry would have been greatly hampered. So God dealt with it. Nothing deals with these issues more profoundly than an extended enslavement in a foreign land.

Envy is a peacetime problem. In times of persecution, it disappears. Persecution has a way of galvanizing saints into a cohesive whole against their common enemy. Thus, persecution will be one of God's foremost ways to deal with envy in the church in the last days.

The captivity was an exceedingly painful period in Israel's history. But it was used strategically of God to remove envy and competitiveness so that, in the end, the nation was restored to a unified entity. And the nation of Israel has never been divided since.

PAUL'S THORN

The apostle Paul had some encounters with God that could have potentially caused others to envy his experiences. But God had a way of dealing with that, which we'll see in a moment. God protects power with problems. That is, when He grants spiritual power to a vessel, He protects His investment in that vessel by keeping him or her humble and dependent through resistance and hassles.

Here's the passage where Paul refers to one of his ecstatic experiences:

> I know a man in Christ who fourteen years ago—whether in the body I do not know, or whether out of the body I do not know, God knows—such a one was caught up to the third heaven. And I know such a man—whether in the body or out of the body I do not know, God knows—how he was caught up into Paradise and heard inexpressible words, which it is not lawful for a man to utter. Of such a one I will boast; yet of myself I will not boast, except in my infirmities. For though I might desire to boast, I will not be a fool; for I will speak the truth. But I refrain, lest anyone should think of me above what he sees me to be or hears from me. And lest I should be

exalted above measure by the abundance of the revelations, a thorn in the flesh was given to me, a messenger of Satan to buffet me, lest I be exalted above measure (2 Corinthians 12:2-7).

Paul's ecstatic experiences and revelations were so powerful that God decided to balance them out with a "thorn in the flesh," lest Paul should be "exalted above measure." When someone has been granted unusual encounters with God, the tendency of other believers is to esteem them more than they ought. Once exalted among believers in that way, that saint becomes a target for envy

we don't typically look at a vessel that's broken and limping and envy it.

from those who desire the same kinds of experiences. So the Lord basically said, "Paul, I've got to deal with the potential of envy from other people as they look at you. So I'm calling you to the Cross. Suffering will keep you from being envied by others."

Paul's thorn in the flesh was a sharing in the sufferings of Christ. It was suffering according to the will of God so that Paul would be received as a servant of the Lord, rather than envied as one of God's favorites. We don't typically look at a vessel that's broken and limping and envy it. Once again, God dealt with the envy issue by impaling His chosen one to the Cross.

ENVYING ANOTHER'S FREEDOM

I relate to the themes of this chapter personally because of the profound suffering I've had to walk through. Let me close this chapter by being honest about my own struggles with envy, but to do so I should probably first tell you a little of my own story.

In 1992, while serving as a pastor of a local church in upstate New York, I suffered a vocal injury that left my voice extremely weak and very painful to use. If I didn't speak, my pain levels were fine; but as soon as I would engage my vocal cords, the pain also engaged. And the more I used my voice, the more it hurt and the weaker I got. I am waiting fervently upon the Lord for my healing, but as of this writing I still am not able to sing. I have since had to resign the pastorate, and I now minister in a limited way by speaking at conferences and churches that are able to accommodate my present restrictions.

The emotional, mental and theological pain of my journey since the injury has been incredibly intense. How could God allow such a devastating thing to happen to me in my prime, when my life was totally dedicated to serving Him? The incapacitation has been traumatic, and finding God in the midst of it has been the great quest of my life. In the midst of the darkness, I have written a number of books that reflect my personal pilgrimage in God. This book is yet another in that ongoing journey.

Before the injury, when I was young and energetic and whole, I suppose that some might have looked at my strengths and abilities and been tempted to be a little envious. But after the injury, all that changed. Instead of possibly being envied, I was now more to be pitied. Now I am like a man who is chained, imprisoned and hindered at every step. I cannot do the things I desire to do but must function within the limitations that are imposed upon me because of this physical affliction. God's promises of release are clear; but until the moment of release comes, the chains are very real.

The chains of my imprisonment have given opportunity for a totally different kind of envy to surface in my soul, a kind of envy I never experienced before the injury. Now, because of my emotional and physical pain levels, I feel like the one who has been crucified. I have set my heart to rejoice to whatever extent my sufferings are a sharing in the sufferings of Christ (see 1 Peter 4:13), but there's no denying the fact that crucifixion is intensely painful. Now the envy issue has taken on a totally new face for me. You see, I've discovered that the brother who is crucified must also deal with envy in his own heart.

Here's how the envy issue impacts me in my present affliction. While being crushed by the Lord, I've been tempted to look at the freedom and joy of those who are seemingly exempt from God's disciplining hand, and I envy their freedoms. I watch others who appear to run and jump with great liberty and joy before the Lord, while I sit in the confines of my cell and chafe against the chains that hinder my movement. I realize the Scripture says to me, "Do not fret because of him who prospers in his way" (Psalm 37:7). And I also realize He says to me, "As many as I love, I rebuke and chasten" (Revelation 3:19). So I know His chastening hand in my life is His love for me; I truly do own that reality. But it's still extremely challenging when you're the one going through the fire to rejoice with those who seem to be experiencing nothing of the purifying fires of God but rather are abounding in strength and blessing and victory.

You're in winter. It's frigid, dried up, barren and dreary. God has shut you down and hemmed you in. And then you look at your brother who is in his spiritual summer. He is bounding free, frolicking in the sunshine of God's favor. He looks at you and wonders what's wrong with you. In that moment of reproach, it's extremely tempting to be envious of your brother's blessings. "Lord, why doesn't my brother experience even a measure of the pruning that I'm experiencing? I know he would look at me differently if he were tasting even a fraction of the cup I'm drinking right now. I'm not asking You to decimate him, but couldn't You level the playing field just a little?"

I must be reminded continually not to look at the path God has given to my brother. If I do, all kinds of carnal things will surface in my soul. So I remember the words of Jesus that He spoke to Peter in reference to John, "If I will that he remain till I come, what is that to you? You follow Me" (John 21:22). In other words, "The path I've chosen for your brother is none of your business. Mind your own business of following Me."

Following Jesus is in itself a full-time employment, requiring undivided focus. If I devote myself to following Jesus, I will not fight as much with envy because I will not be comparing my journey with someone else's. Although I may struggle at times with my lot in life, one day I will fully understand the wisdom of the course God has set before my feet.

CHAPTER 7

PERCEIVING THE "MEASURE OF GRACE"

PREVIOUSLY we said that GOD deals with envy by taking His chosen vessel through such an excruciating journey that the brothers' envy is melted into pity. While that is true, it doesn't address the matter of our own personal responsibility to deal with the envy of our own hearts when we see it. Let's look at some principles that will help us do battle in the war zones of our hearts so that we might please our beloved Savior who has given His life for us.

Envy, in the final analysis, is our own responsibility before God. We must deal with it forcefully and immediately. Since envy is a hider, it can sometimes operate in our hearts for months and even years without us even being aware of it. But the

Lord has ways of bringing the impurities to the surface, so we can see them. When He turns up the fire in our lives, the impurities rise to the surface where they can be identified. Once we see the issues, it's crucial that we repent and do business with God.

One of the most effective things we can do to deal with envy is simply admit its presence. Great power is released when we bring our sins into the light. Once God shows us the envy of our

> ### ONE of THE most effective THINGS
> we can do to deal with envy is
> ### simply admit its presence.

hearts and we confess it humbly before Him, we are doing what 2 Timothy 2:19 refers to as departing from iniquity. Our faithfulness to deal with issues like envy, once they are surfaced through God's fiery dealings, empowers us to become "vessels of gold and silver" (2 Timothy 2:20) that are being purified through true repentance. When we thus cleanse ourselves from our iniquities, we become "a vessel for honor, sanctified and useful for the Master, prepared for every good work" (2 Timothy 2:21).

THE WEANING PROCESS

Psalm 131 points to a dynamic that is very relevant to our discussion:

> LORD, my heart is not haughty, nor my eyes lofty. Neither do I concern myself with great matters, nor with things too profound for me. Surely I have calmed and quieted my soul, like a weaned child with his mother; like a weaned child is my soul within me (Psalm 131:1-2).

David is dealing in this psalm with the issue of ambition, which is the seedbed of envy. Envy happens when, after setting our heart or eye upon a lofty goal, one of our brothers moves toward that goal more quickly than we do. The problem is not only that our brother is gaining higher ground but also that we have set our aspirations on lofty things when we should have been content with what we have (see 1 Timothy 6:6-8). It certainly is right to set our heart upon the upward call of God in Christ (see Philippians 3:14), but there are "lofty" and "haughty" heights that are beyond what we should desire. Once we begin to aspire to "things too profound" for us, we cannot live at peace with our current attainments. When thus motivated by ambition, we become easy targets for envy (when we see someone else attaining what we've aspired).

The desire for greatness is like the infantile longings of a child who wants his mother's milk. The longings are real; but if satisfied, they will keep the child at an infantile level of maturity.

In order to graduate the child to solid food that will be more nutritional and strengthening, the mother weans the baby from his infantile dependence upon milk. *Weaning involves withholding from the child what he desires.* This produces great anxiety in the child, who remonstrates and throws a tantrum. Eventually, however, the child wearies and settles back into a reluctant acceptance of the fact that no amount of hollering is going to bring what he desires. For reasons outside his control, the parent is withholding the object desired.

Once the weaning is complete, the child is able to resume a quiet, serene, even satisfied demeanor. Why? Because through the weaning process the child's appetites have been changed. By the withholding of the mother's milk, the child no longer craves what he once craved. Here's the operative principle of weaning: *Withholding changes the appetite.* In weaning us, God withholds what we want in order to change our desires.

A weaned child is one who has allowed his parents to shape his appetites.

When our hearts are set upon lofty, ambitious desires that are too profound for us, God withholds from us the very things we desire. At first we're frustrated because we're convinced our high aspirations are part of the God-given vision to which we are called. Our frustration turns to anger and then to heartache. Throughout the entire process, if another brother attains what we wanted, envy crouches at our door. If the Lord withholds from us long enough, however, eventually we will stop craving the thing we once desired. Once our hearts are settled in the portion God has given us, we are said to be weaned.

IN WEANING US, GOD WITHHOLDS WHAT WE WANT IN ORDER TO CHANGE OUR DESIRES.

God is portrayed in Psalm 131 as a loving, nursing mother. The maternal care of God for His children is compelling and real. The Lord weans us tenderly and with deep affections.

Weaning is a process, happening in stages. First the child is weaned from the mother's breast, then from the bottle and then sometimes from a pacifier, or "soother." It can also happen repeatedly throughout our lives as God deals with different issues. He'll wean us now from one thing; next year He'll wean us from something else. Ambition-driven envy is only one of many infantile, carnal desires from which God will wean us.

Even though it was 18 years ago, I still remember when we weaned our firstborn. Joel loved to nurse, but he *really* loved his bottle! He was weaned from nursing fairly easily, but weaning him from the bottle was another matter entirely. When we withheld the bottle from him, his first response was anger. But when, over time, he finally realized that the bottle was never going to be given to him again, his yelling turned to wailing and he began to mourn with heart-wrenching sobs. I remember that Marci and I were brought to the edge of tears just by watching him grieve over the loss of his bottle. It was traumatic for our entire household! Our hearts ached to fulfill his desire, and yet we refused to give it to him because of our love for him. Such are the affections of our heavenly Father toward us during our weaning process.

The Lord has withheld from me areas of valid ministry, and I have wept for them with many tears. But in those times when my spirit rises up in perspective, I am able to see that His kindness has kept me from ministry involvements that would have limited me to a more immature or parochial function. Through the weaning, He is helping to shape my desires so that I might grow up into a more mature level. My prayer is that I will mature to the place where I no longer desire what He chooses to give another but will be satisfied in the pursuit of all Christ has destined for my life.

Notice that David wrote "like a weaned child with his mother." The weaning process is intrinsically wrapped up in the child's relationship with his mother. It is the mother's loving assurances that help the child to process what is happening. What brings the baby through is the mother/child connection.

When God is weaning us of our personal agendas, He withholds what we want, but at the same time He clutches us to His breast. Even though He seems to be acting as our opponent, His nearness is incredibly sweet and assuring. In fact, He will use the weaning process to establish us even further in His love for us. It is thus, in the affections of His love, that He empowers us to overcome the ambition-driven envy of our hearts and to come to rest in His love.

ENVY AT THE LOCAL CHURCH LEVEL

The first thing we can do to deal with the envy of our hearts is to allow God to shape our desires through the weaning process. Secondly, we can pursue the greatness of Christ's love. It is written, "Love does not envy" (1 Corinthians 13:4). So the greatest deterrent to envy is love. When we are perfected in love, we will no longer envy each other.

Paul also wrote, "And if one member suffers, all the members suffer with it; or if one member is honored, all the members rejoice with it" (1 Corinthians 12:26). If someone in our local church is suffering, it's comparatively easy to come alongside that person and suffer with them, weep with them and comfort

the greatest deterrent to envy is Love.

them. But "if one member is honored"—well, that's a different story. If the pastor honors another member but doesn't honor you—wow!—it's amazing how envy can appear suddenly out of nowhere. The test of envy is not when another member suffers but when he or she is honored. Am I able to "rejoice with" that member who is honored? Can I rejoice when the church down the street prospers? Whenever I envy another member in the body, it's because my love is not perfect and complete. Those who love do not envy.

We are exhorted in Scripture, "Pursue love, and desire spiritual gifts, but especially that you may prophesy" (1 Corinthians 14:1). It's right to desire to be used by God, but sometimes we turn that into a desire to be given a platform for public ministry. We begin to desire position. Then when someone else gets the position or recognition we wanted, we lose our love and fall back into envy. When we envy another's placement, we lose perspective on how wonderfully the Lord has been using us. If we will just get busy in the great harvest of God, laboring in the harvest has a way of equalizing a lot of things in our souls. When the heat of gathering the harvest is high, we don't care how much another is harvesting; we simply rejoice that we don't have to gather the whole harvest all by ourselves! It's vital that we transition from a platform mentality to a harvest mentality. In the harvest, we minister in the sight of God alone. When we learn the secret of living for an audience of One, envy will no longer be an issue.

WHEN WE LEARN THE SECRET OF LIVING FOR AN AUDIENCE OF ONE, ENVY WILL NO LONGER BE AN ISSUE.

Those who minister to the bride of Christ are said to be "one": "Now he who plants and he who waters *are one*, and each one will receive his own reward according to his own labor" (1 Corinthians 3:8, emphasis added). The one who plants and the one who waters in the same field (local church) are not competing with each other. They are on the same team, laboring toward the same end, and so are said to be one. Apostles, prophets, evangelists, pastors, teachers, equippers, encouragers, servers—all are one. Your success is my success. If competition ever arises between ministers, it is because we've forgotten that we're joined to one another. Competitiveness in ministry immobilizes and hamstrings the advance of the Kingdom in our midst because it's the body working against itself.

We can take a lesson from a very humble creature in the Bible. "There are four things which are little on the earth, but they are exceedingly wise" (Proverbs 30:24). The four creatures cited are the ant, the rock badger, the locust and the spider. Look what it says about the locusts: "The locusts have no king, yet they all advance in ranks" (v. 27). The locusts are esteemed as "exceedingly wise" because of their ability to unify around a common pursuit. In other words, they are exceedingly wise because there is no envy in their ranks. Ah, what wisdom! They stay together, not

> COMPETITIVENESS IN MINISTRY IMMOBILIZES AND HAMSTRINGS THE ADVANCE OF THE KINGDOM IN OUR MIDST BECAUSE IT'S THE BODY WORKING AGAINST ITSELF.

because they are drawn by the magnetism of a primary leader, but because they are galvanized by a community vision. They stay together by honoring one another. May we be wise enough in this critical hour to push aside all envy, competition or personal ambition and exercise the spiritual grace of preferring one another in love. Let's get in rank with our brothers and sisters and advance together in our common pursuit of the harvest!

Psalm 16:3 contains one of the most beautiful declarations of Scripture: "As for the saints who are on the earth, 'They are the excellent ones, in whom is all my delight.'" When someone else in my community of believers excels in any pursuit, may my instinctive response be that he or she is the object of "all my delight." When we view each other in this way, the body of Christ will edify itself in love, growing up into the head—who is Christ (see Ephesians 4:13-16).

ENVY AT THE TRANSLOCAL CHURCH LEVEL

While envy is a serious problem within local churches, it is an even more serious issue between local churches. And as we've said, it's often between the brothers (leaders—both male and female) of those churches.

I don't know a single leader who enjoys admitting that he struggles with envy toward his fellow leaders. Envy, competition, ambition—nothing is disclaimed and disowned more passionately by ministry leaders. And yet for all our denials, the deadly threads of envy continue to weave their diabolical work throughout the church of Jesus Christ, breeding suspicion, distrust and separation. So while there's nothing more painful to talk about than envy, the urgency we feel to reclaim the unity of the body of Christ compels us to face the issues with honesty.

Often the tiny tinge of pain we feel over the success of another church or ministry is so wispy and passing that we don't even recognize its presence. But with envy, one principle is particularly true: "A little leaven leavens the whole lump" (Galatians 5:9). It only takes the slightest, almost imperceptible amount of envy to discolor our entire souls.

Jesus sets up His kingdom in such a way that if envy is in the heart, it is almost certain to find occasion to rise up.

Now I am going to delve into what is probably the most tender, sensitive subject matter of this entire book: the manner in which God has invested varying degrees of ministry effectiveness and influence to His leaders in the body of Christ. By anointing His leaders at different levels, God has rigged the thing so that every opportunity for envy can easily present itself in our hearts. He simply will not allow us to hide from the issue.

I have looked with considerable fascination at the manner in which David surrounded himself with men to whom he gave various levels of recognition, authority and reward. Below David was Joab, the captain of the army; below Joab were three mighty men; below the three mighty men was a second and lesser group of three mighty men; then below them was a grouping of 30 mighty men; then after the 30 came all the brave soldiers of David's ranks. I'm thinking to myself, *Lord, isn't this kind of multilevel ranking a deadly way to guarantee that envy will infiltrate the entire army?* The answer seems to be that God doesn't shy away from giving us opportunity to envy. In fact, He sets up His kingdom in such a way that if envy is in the heart, it is almost certain to find occasion to rise up. The One who has given different degrees of grace to the various members of the body seems to have no qualms about saying, "This one is to be over this sphere, and that one is to serve over that sphere."

God has unapologetically given varying measures of grace to the members in the body and then has called us to honor one another by joining together for a common cause. If we get in the flesh and begin to compare and envy, He calls us to repent and demonstrate the fruits of repentance.

It seems that Jesus did something similar with the disciples. From among the crowds, He sent out 70; from among the 70 there were 12 who were called to follow Him everywhere; from among the 12, three were chosen to accompany Jesus to some of His most glorious demonstrations of power and glory; and of the three, one was said to be "the disciple whom He loved" (John 19:26). It appears that Jesus' way of rewarding faithfulness and love was by choosing a small group from the larger group for special experiences and understanding. But such rewards always carry the risk of inducing envy in the immature who are not chosen for the select smaller group. Jesus seems to have designed His kingdom in a way that gives envy its maximum opportunity to surface—so that we can deal with it.

It's my observation that David's mighty men find a contemporary counterpart in the pastors or senior leaders of churches and related ministries. There is no question that God has given varying amounts of grace and differing orbs of influence to His leaders. The whole issue of envy enters when leaders begin to compare their grace and sphere with that of others. When God's mighty men get together, it becomes a great question whether or not they will be able to recognize and honor the measure of grace that rests upon each one.

To understand the term "the measure of grace," we need to understand the two distinct definitions of "grace" in the New Testament. First, "grace" is often defined as "unmerited favor." In this sense, grace is used to describe God's kindness in granting us salvation by faith, totally apart from works or effort on our part (see Ephesians 2:8 as an example). This has also been termed "saving grace." The second Bible meaning of "grace" is also common, however, and it refers to the enablement of God through the Holy Spirit that empowers the believer to do the will of God. This "empowering grace" is what Paul had in mind when he wrote, "But by the grace of God I am what I am, and His grace toward me was not in vain; but I labored more abundantly than they all, yet not I, but the grace of God which was with me" (1 Corinthians 15:10). It is this second aspect of grace—this enabling power—to which we refer in this chapter when we speak of "the measure of grace."

VARYING MEASURES OF GRACE

When a group of pastors from a region gather for fellowship, there is an amazing assortment of interrelational dynamics exploding all over the room all at the same time. Everybody is checking everyone else out. While some have worked past what I'm about to describe, some have not. Although pastors rarely come right out and ask each other, what they really want to know of one another is, How many people are attending your church now, and how much momentum do you have in your ministry? The answers to these and other questions help leaders in a room determine who carries more or less weight in the church world.

I hope you don't think I'm being cynical. I'm simply being honest about what the Lord has shown me about my own heart, and I don't think I'm the only one who has related to other believers in this way. The Lord dealt very strongly with me about how I would rate my fellow pastors in relation to myself as "equal," "below" or "above" what I perceived myself to be. When I saw how I was doing this subconsciously in my soul, I had to repent very seriously before the Lord.

We all know it, but let's establish this truth for the purposes of this book: There is no pecking order in the kingdom of God. There are no people who are lesser or greater. We all have equal value and merit before the throne as children of God. We are all equally loved and cherished by our Beloved. Period.

However, we do have varying degrees of grace upon our lives. Some have more grace from God than others. Don't ask me why; ask Him. He has simply chosen to pour out varying amounts of grace upon His leaders. To His Son, Jesus Christ, He gave the anointing of the Spirit without measure: "For He whom God has sent speaks the words of God, for God does not give the Spirit by measure" (John 3:34). The rest of us receive an anointing in a measure: "But to each one of us grace was given according to the measure of Christ's gift" (Ephesians 4:7).

Perceiving the Grace on Someone

If we are to overcome envy between ministry leaders in the body of Christ, one of the things we must learn is how to properly perceive the grace of God that rests upon another minister of the gospel.

Paul pointed to this dynamic when he wrote about his relationship to the apostles in Jerusalem. When they first met, the apostles scrutinized Paul and evaluated the genuineness of his conversion and calling. Paul writes of this encounter by saying, "When James, Cephas, and John, who seemed to be pillars, perceived the grace that had been given to me, they gave me and Barnabas the right hand of fellowship, that we should go to the Gentiles and they to the circumcised" (Galatians 2:9). James, Peter and John took some considerable time with Paul so that they might perceive the grace that was on his life. When they shared with him, their hearts burned with the same fire that was in Paul's heart and they were able to discern the genuineness of the grace God had bestowed upon him. Once they had perceived that grace, they were able to extend the right hand of fellowship and to release Paul to function in his sphere. Fellowship (or the giving of the right hand of fellowship) among the apostles flowed out of a recognition of the grace each one had received.

On one occasion I was asking a personal friend who is pastor of a large church in Europe about the dynamics of inter-church unity in his city. As is so often the case when I ask that kind of question in my travels, his response was not very encouraging. One of the interesting dynamics of this ministry at the time was that God had raised up this church very rapidly in the city, and it had quickly become the largest evangelical church there. All the other churches of similar emphasis and style were substantially smaller, which in turn fueled envy in the hearts of the other pastors of the city. So the spirit that existed between the brothers of the city was not even close to being unified. As we were discussing this, my friend made a fascinating point. He said, "For unity to exist among leaders in a city, they must be willing to recognize the grace that God has given each one. But that's not enough. They must also be willing to recognize the *measure* of the grace that God has given each one."

The apostles didn't simply perceive the grace upon Paul's life; they perceived *the measure of grace* upon his life. When they saw the measure of grace given to Paul, they had no problem acknowledging him as a brother, extending the right hand of fellowship to him and releasing him to his call to the Gentiles. In other words, it was their recognition of the measure of grace on his life that empowered them to walk in unity together.

The measure of grace on someone's life is sovereignly determined by God. "A man can receive nothing unless it has been given to him from heaven" (John 3:27). When God sovereignly gives a gift to one of His servants, none of us has the right to question or envy that gifting. We cannot have unity where there are jealousies and competitions over the measure of grace given to various ones. God cannot allow the blessing of unity to fall (see Psalm 133) until we have dealt with these issues violently in our hearts.

OUR SPIRITUAL DESTINY OFTEN HANGS IN THE BALANCE OF WHETHER WE CAN RECOGNIZE AND HONOR THAT WHICH HEAVEN HAS GIVEN OTHERS IN THE BODY OF CHRIST.

When we perceive the measure of grace upon another pastor, church or ministry leader, we are taking a giant step toward conquering envy, because we recognize the grace on their life was given to them on no merit of their own; it was the sovereign choosing of God. They did nothing to earn or deserve it. It is Christ's gift to them, and we acknowledge it with gratefulness in our hearts to God.

That which is from God must be honored. When I perceive that another has received something from God, I must honor and respect and support the authenticity of what God is doing in and through the other's life. When the Pharisees would not honor the baptism God had given John, they were terribly impoverished for it. John had received something from heaven, but they had rejected it. In turn, when Jesus came along, it was John's turn to be tested. Would he be able to honor the grace that was upon Jesus' life? (He passed the test.) Our spiritual destiny often hangs in the balance of whether we can recognize and honor that which heaven has given others in the body of Christ.

My pride doesn't want to concede that someone else might have been given a greater measure of grace than me. (In actuality, envy is rooted in pride.) When I encounter someone with a greater sphere than mine, my flesh wants to respond with all kinds of weird attitudes. It takes a largeness of heart to say, "That person has a greater grace from God on his life than I have." It takes an even greater largeness of heart to rejoice in that grace on his life.

A person has to work through some flesh issues to joyfully submit to someone with great grace on their lives. Barnabas's relationship to Paul is intriguing along these lines. When the two got started in ministry together, Barnabas was the big brother and Paul was the little brother. Barnabas was the leader; Paul was the assistant. But there was greater grace on Paul's life than Barnabas's, and it soon became evident as they traveled in ministry. Before long, Paul had stepped forward into the place of leadership and Barnabas had become the assistant. Now, that's a tough transition to weather!

Everything shook down when a difference of opinion arose between them. Barnabas wanted to take John Mark on the next ministry trip, but Paul refused. If Barnabas had started out *under* Paul, it would have been different; but he started out *over* Paul. Because of how their relationship had evolved, Barnabas was unable to acquiesce to Paul's leadership. His inability to receive Paul's leadership meant that they would part ways and become two missionary parties (which was actually God's will all along). As a result, however, we never again hear in the New Testament about Barnabas's ministry, its nature or its effectiveness. God still used Barnabas mightily, no doubt, but the Holy Spirit went on to chronicle the mighty acts accomplished through the vessel with the greater grace on his life (Paul). So you have to decide if you want to join Paul and ride the wave or part ways and go a different path (which is fine by God too).

DEFINING SPHERES OF MINISTRY

This next principle is extremely important: The measure of grace upon a leader's life will determine the measure of his or her sphere. "Sphere" becomes an all-important word in our present discussion, denoting the extent of one's authority and influence

> ### THE measure of grace upon a LEADER's LIfe wILL Determine THE measure of HIS OR HER spHeRe.

in ministry. God gives grace to each one. The manner in which we faithfully exercise that grace will determine the extent of our ministry sphere.

It was the measure of grace on Paul's life that determined his sphere. He wrote:

> We, however, will not boast beyond measure, but within the limits of the sphere which God appointed us—a sphere which especially includes you . . . not boasting of things beyond measure, that is, in other men's labors, but having hope, that as your faith is increased, we shall be greatly enlarged by you in our sphere (2 Corinthians 10:13-15).

God had given Paul the grace to minister to the Corinthian believers, and now because of the history of their relationship through grace, they were recognized as falling within Paul's sphere of ministry authority.

Each servant of God has a sphere of ministry authority that is varied according to the measure of grace each one has received and the degree to which they labor in it. However, Paul acknowledged that even the intensity with which he labored was because of the empowering grace of God on his life: "But by the grace of God I am what I am, and His grace toward me was not in vain; but I labored more abundantly than they all, yet not I, but the grace of God which was with me" (1 Corinthians 15:10). So one's sphere of ministry influence grows as one is faithful to minister according to the grace on one's life.

SpHeRe Has to do witH HoRizontaL bReadth of infLuence and authoRity.

When we properly discern the measure of grace on someone's life, we are able to honor the sphere God has given that person. Sphere has to do with horizontal breadth of influence and authority. It is not a vertical pecking order but a horizontal influence. When a pebble is dropped into a pond, the larger the pebble, the greater the ripple effect. The ripple effect could be likened unto one's sphere. God gives each one of us our own ripple effect (sphere) in the body of Christ. Some servants of God make bigger ripples in the body of Christ than others. Because of the anointing and grace on their life, they leave a deeper, longer-lasting impact on the saints of God. Some servants will bless a home group; some will bless a church; some will shake a church; some will shake a city; some will shake a nation; some will shake many nations. It all has to do with the measure of grace given to the vessel. The measure of grace determines the degree of ministry

impact, which in turn will create a sphere of influence and authority within which that leader is recognized and honored.

Sphere has nothing to do with placement within an organi-
zation or religious structure. Jesus held no ecclesiastical position
during His earthly ministry and yet there was no stopping the
sphere of His ministry. No human title can enhance your sphere,
nor can the lack of human recognition detract from your sphere.
No one can limit your sphere! It is God given, and it's yours. And
it can change and grow over time. As we cooperate with God's
grace, He will sometimes launch us into greater spheres of ministry influence. And if we walk carelessly, He can draw back the
lines of our sphere.

One of the great mistakes sometimes made in the body of
Christ is the unspoken assumption that if I honor and release
you to your sphere, I will lose some of my authority in my
sphere. Not only is this false thinking, but it also will produce a
horrible tide of envy in the body of Christ. It is a lie that says
I must limit or deny you your sphere in order to protect mine.
Paul appealed to the Corinthian believers "that as your faith is

IT IS A LIE THAT SAYS I MUST LIMIT
OR DENY YOU YOUR SPHERE IN ORDER
TO PROTECT MINE.

increased, we shall be greatly enlarged by you in our sphere"
(2 Corinthians 10:15). He is saying to them, "If you can stretch
your faith to believe this, you will actually benefit from greatly
enlarging us in our sphere over you. You might be tempted to
think that if you enlarge our sphere of influence over you that
you will lose something; but in fact, you will gain tremendously.
By enlarging us in our sphere over you, you will find that our
apostolic ministry in your midst will pave the way for greater

ministry opportunities for you than you could have ever produced on your own."

We will always benefit most when we release each other to
our respective spheres—yea, when we campaign for the fullness
of each other's spheres! We have a tendency to think that there
is room for only so many ripples in our pond. The truth is, we
aren't in a pond; we're in an *ocean* of worldwide heartache and
suffering. The ocean of human need about us is inexhaustible,
and there's plenty of room for everyone's ripple to have its full
extent of influence and blessing. Unfortunately, because of their
insecurities, some leaders function as though they're in a pond
and there's not room for much more than their own ripples.
Such leaders will always have a limited orb of ministry impact.

Influencing Tens, Hundreds, Thousands

To use yet another scriptural analogy of the principle of sphere,
the Bible talks about the dividing of the nation of Israel into
groups of tens, fifties, hundreds and thousands. This is the
advice Jethro gave Moses when he saw how overworked Moses
was:

> Moreover you shall select from all the people able men,
> such as fear God, men of truth, hating covetousness; and
> place such over them to be rulers of thousands, rulers of
> hundreds, rulers of fifties, and rulers of tens (Exodus
> 18:21).

So some rulers had a sphere over tens of people, while other
rulers had a sphere over thousands. David picked up on the
same principle, for it says, "And David numbered the people who
were with him, and set captains of thousands and captains
of hundreds over them" (2 Samuel 18:1.) David gave to some
captains a greater sphere than to others.

The Son of David still gives greater spheres to some than to others. Those with discernment can see it. The women of Israel were able to see the difference between what God had given to David and what God had given to Saul. So when David and the warriors came back from the battle with the Philistines, the women sang a song about David's greater sphere.

So the women sang as they danced, and said: "Saul has slain his thousands, and David his ten thousands." Then Saul was very angry, and the saying displeased him; and he said, "They have ascribed to David ten thousands, and to me they have ascribed only thousands. Now what more can he have but the kingdom?" So Saul eyed David from that day forward (1 Samuel 18:7-9).

Both Saul and David were anointed by God; but these women discerned that the anointing on David's life was greater, for he had been granted a sphere of "ten thousands" whereas Saul had been granted a sphere of "thousands." David's greater sphere was evidenced by his ability to kill the Philistine champion that Saul

if Saul had been secure in his identity, he could have fathered a young man with a sphere greater than his own.

couldn't kill. When they accurately discerned David's greater sphere, it caused envy to explode within Saul's heart (because of insecurity), an envy he harbored to the day of his death. Saul assumed that if he released David to his sphere, his own sphere would be threatened and compromised. He equated sphere with hierarchical position—the throne—reasoning that only one man can sit on the throne at one time. By equating sphere with position, he reasoned that David was his rival for the throne. He didn't realize that he could have enjoyed the throne while releasing David to the fullness of his sphere in God. If Saul had been secure in his identity, he could have fathered a young man with a sphere greater than his own. He missed a marvelous opportunity for thrilling spiritual fatherhood.

Accurately Assessing Your Own Sphere

Even before we can accurately perceive the sphere of another, I believe we need to cultivate the grace of perceiving our own sphere accurately. Only then can we relate to another's sphere, even as James, Cephas and John were able to relate in freedom to Paul's sphere. They knew their own sphere, so they could honor Paul's sphere accordingly.

There arise several important questions to ask ourselves: *Am I a humble saint in the army? Am I a ruler of tens? Of hundreds? Of thousands? Or a ruler (as was David) of ten thousands? Do I have the security and wisdom to make an accurate self-assessment of my sphere in the body of Christ?* (At least for the present, recognizing that our sphere can both increase and diminish.) Only if I'm accurate in my self-assessment will I be able to accurately perceive the measure of grace upon another. Said another way, to the degree that I am self-deceived about the grace on my life, to that degree I will be unable to accurately perceive the grace on the lives of others.

One of the virtues my wife and I have tried to cultivate in our children is the ability to accurately evaluate their strengths and weaknesses. When, for example, they have fantasized themselves into being a better basketball player than they really are, we've tried to help them embrace reality. And when they have allowed their insecurities to hold them back from their potential, we have spoken assurances to them: "You can do it!" We want them to value the ability to make truthful assessments of their giftings and abilities. We have watched other parents who have not helped their children find the balance between excess and defect, and it sets their kids up for disappointment. If our kids can learn to accurately evaluate themselves, perhaps they will grow in the grace of perceiving their own sphere and the spheres of others in the body of Christ.

As parents guide their children to an accurate self-assessment, even so all of us need the wise input of faithful friends who will reflect to us in honesty and loyalty the perspectives that will keep us from becoming skewed or inflated regarding our self-discernment. Countless numbers of leaders could have been saved from shipwreck had they humbly submitted to those who endeavored to bring loving correction and helpful feedback to them.

an accurate self-assessment of our sphere empowers us to relate to our brothers and sisters with a free spirit.

Romans 12:3 calls us not to think too highly of ourselves, nor to think too meanly of ourselves: "For I say, through the grace given to me, to everyone who is among you, not to think of himself more highly than he ought to think, but to think soberly, as God has dealt to each one a measure of faith."

"To think soberly" includes the necessity of not thinking too little of ourselves, which would not be according to faith. Paul is essentially saying, "Allow the grace of God to help you find a humble yet faith-inspired self-assessment of your giftings, measure of grace and sphere of ministry."

I know leaders in the body of Christ who are constantly tripping up because they have not been able to accurately evaluate themselves. They haven't come to see how their weaknesses are working against them, so they haven't learned to allow others to make up for those weaknesses and help them. Thus, their sphere is constantly hampered by their insecurities and unresolved liabilities.

An accurate self-assessment of our sphere empowers us to relate to our brothers and sisters with a free spirit. It gives us a free heart to relate openhandedly with those whose sphere is lesser or greater than our own. Here is where envy is deflated. Because I know the goodness and calling of God in my own life, I am able to celebrate the goodness and calling of God in your life. Hallelujah!

WHERE NO ONE IS YOUR COMPETITOR

Paul had a grand pursuit toward which he ran with great zeal—the pursuit of the knowledge of Christ. He recognized that in this race he was running, not against other believers, but against the standard of the call that God had placed before him personally. His only competitor was himself. This is why he wrote,

> Brethren, I do not count myself to have apprehended; but one thing I do, forgetting those things which are behind and reaching forward to those things which are ahead, I press toward the goal for the prize of the upward call of God in Christ Jesus (Philippians 3:13-14).

Let me suggest this thought: Set your heart on a playing field where no one is your competitor.

How do we do that? I believe Colossians 3:2 holds an answer for us. "Set your mind on things above, not on things on the earth." When setting goals for your life, articulate them in terms of heavenly realities. In contrast to that, we are usually taught to articulate our goals in earthly terms:

- My goal is for my ministry to double in its reach this year.
- My goal is for my home group to multiply three times in the next five years.
- My goal is to get my doctorate by the time I'm 30.
- My goal is to establish a new church in this community.
- My goal is to support twice as many missionaries by this time next year.

While all of those goals appear noble, they are goals on an earthly playing field where others can compete. Where there is room for competition between brothers, there is room for self-seeking and envy. What would happen, rather, if we set goals upon heavenly pursuits for ourselves, where no one can compete?

- My goal is to take the lowest place at the marriage supper of the Lamb and to be called higher because the Bridegroom calls me His friend.
- My goal is to stand before the judgment seat of Christ with much gold, silver and precious stones to present to Him.
- My goal is to be known in heaven.
- My goal is to be great in the sight of God when I stand before Christ without fault and with great glory.
- My goal is to stand before God's throne with many other souls surrounding me, of whom I might be able to say to Christ, "Here am I and the children whom God has given Me."
- My goal is to hear these simple words: "Well done, good and faithful servant."

We need to set goals for our lives such that, even though we be thrown into prison like Joseph or Paul, our goals can still be pursued. When Paul wrote, "Set your mind on things above, not on things on the earth" (Colossians 3:2), I think he was saying, "Set your affections, your aspirations, your goals, your inner longings, on things above." When our inner aspirations are upon an upward calling with which no one can interfere or compete, our hearts will be amazingly free from the seductive tentacles of envy.

CHAPTER 8

THE ENVY DETOUR: DEATH OR DESTINY

ONE OF THE MOST SINKING FEELINGS YOU CAN HAVE when you're hurriedly driving to something important is to encounter the road sign Detour. Something inside goes, "Oh, no!" I think we all hate detours. And yet I've discovered something about God: He is a God of detours. Whenever He takes us the long way around, it is always for a purpose, even if we can't see it at the time.

This truth is illustrated powerfully in one segment of Israel's journey through the wilderness. We have something to learn by looking at a detour in their journey that was very strategic in God's purposes.

The 40 years of the nation's wanderings in the wilderness had drawn to a close and it was time to move forward into Canaan.

So Moses asked the king of Edom if they could pass through Edom's territory. Edom was the name given to the nation of Esau's descendants. Edom was Israel's brother, and the Edomites still carried a lot of bitterness toward the Israelites because of Jacob's trickery toward Esau. In a word, Edom was envious of Israel. When Moses asked for passage through Edom's territory, the king of Edom flatly denied the request. So the children of Israel continued to move in a northerly direction, passing along Edom's western border (see Numbers 20:14-21).

HORMAH REPRESENTS FOR US AN EARLY VICTORY THAT PRECEDES A LONG DETOUR.

They approached a point just south of the Dead Sea when suddenly they were attacked by a king from Canaan—the king of Arad—who took some of the people as prisoners. After prayer, the Israelites attacked this Canaanite king and not only defeated the Canaanites but also destroyed them and their cities. The chief battleground was a place called Hormah (see Numbers 21:1-3). Hormah represents for us an early victory that precedes a long detour.

Even though not many people today realize it, the taking of Jericho was *not* Israel's first entry into the Promised Land. Their first Canaanite victory was actually here at Hormah. They penetrated Canaan territory as far as Hormah, coming to within roughly 40 miles of Jerusalem.

From this vantage, Canaan—their inheritance—lay before them. The door was wide open. All they had to do was keep moving north. But before taking the next step, they decided to pause and seek God's counsel. "Lord, which Canaanite city should we conquer next?"

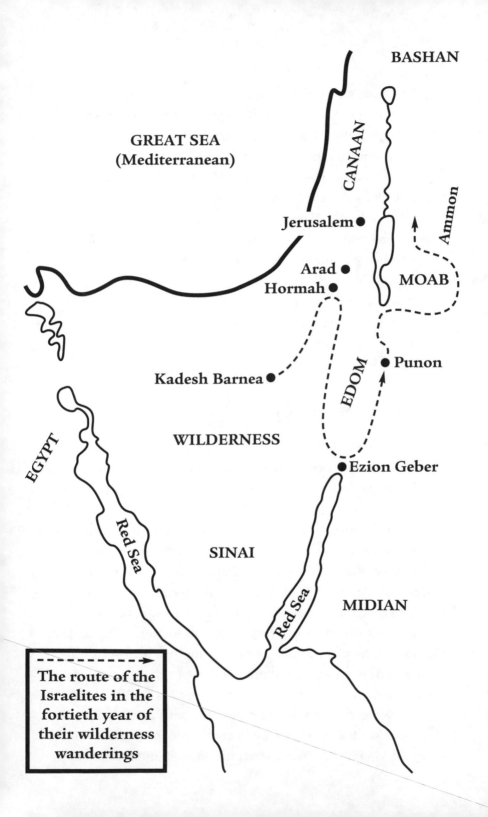

BASHAN

GREAT SEA
(Mediterranean)

CANAAN

Jerusalem ●

Arad ●
Hormah ●

Ammon

MOAB

Punon
EDOM

Kadesh Barnea ●

WILDERNESS

Ezion Geber

EGYPT

Red Sea

SINAI

Red Sea

MIDIAN

- - - - - - - ▶
The route of the
Israelites in the
fortieth year of
their wilderness
wanderings

The Lord's answer stunned them: "Turn around, retreat out of Canaan, go all the way back to the Red Sea, and then make your way around Edom's eastern border."

I can imagine them thinking, *Lord, You have got to be kidding! We are in Canaan! This is our Promised Land. Why can't we just keep going? Why are You telling us to go all the way back to the Red Sea? Come on!* But the Lord's directive was very clear to Moses, so the people turned and went back toward the Red Sea (see Numbers 21:4). They circumvented Edom's southern border and then began to move back north around Edom's east side—all this so they would not have to pass through Edom's territory. Talk about a major detour! (Follow the arrows on the map to see what appears to have been their route.)

ISRAEL AND EDOM

The reason for the detour, in a word, was Edom. Edom had an ancient root of envy toward his brother, Israel, so God had to lead the Israelites in a way that responded properly to Edom's envy. God had to give Israel his inheritance without exacerbating Edom's envy inordinately. I can imagine the Lord saying, "Don't start to grumble about the long path I'm taking you on right now. Because if you get Canaan too easily, the envy of Edom will erupt and they will challenge your victory. Take Canaan now and Edom will come and attack you. But if you will walk faithfully through this torturous detour, the envy of Edom will be placated; and when I bring you into your inheritance, your brother, Edom, will not come to challenge your new territory."

However, God was dealing not only with Edom's envy; but He was also dealing with Israel's ambitious spirit. Their victory over the king of Arad was a sweeping success, and the ease of the battle put a gleam in their eye. They had tasted victory and it tasted very good! Now they had visions of the land melting before them like butter. An ambitious, conquering spirit arose in their hearts. "Okay, Edom, if you're not going to let us pass through your territory, then watch this. We'll just move directly into Canaan for ourselves and show you a thing or two. Watch our war machine in action, brother, and eat your heart out!" While this attitude is not articulated in the text, I am suggesting it was there because of the common human propensity to adopt a triumphal spirit in the wake of success.

You may recall that Esau (Edom) and Jacob were twin brothers and rivals right from the start. Esau sold his birthright to Jacob for some food (see Genesis 25:29-34) and then was tricked out of his father's blessing when Jacob pretended to be Esau and deceptively stole the blessing that was intended for Esau (see Genesis 27). The nation of Edom never forgot this. Instead of taking responsibility for the lack of blessing on his life, Esau thought it was all Jacob's fault. Even though centuries had elapsed, the rivalry between the two nations was still alive and well.

Because Esau didn't take personal responsibility for his relationship with God, his descendants ended up sinning grossly against Israel. In response, God declared that He would judge the nation of Edom. One of the prophets who recorded God's wrath against Edom was a prophet who wrote one of the shortest books of the Bible, the prophet Obadiah.

The book of Obadiah is an exposé on envy, dealing specifically with Esau's relationship with his brother, Jacob. Esau's envy caused him to distance himself from Jacob and the promises to the patriarchs. Edom became a nation that, instead of participating in the kingdom of God, persecuted it. The fruit of envy is laid bare in the book of Obadiah, revealing the following principles regarding envy's consequences:

- *Envy leads to perverted thinking and loss of understanding.*

  "'Will I not in that day,' says the LORD, 'even destroy the wise men from Edom, and understanding from the mountains of Esau?'" (Obadiah 1:8). When we refuse to deal with envy in our hearts, our thinking processes become twisted and we fall into deception.

- *Envy will cause us to side with those who are opposed to the purposes of God.*

  "In the day that you stood on the other side—in the day that strangers carried captive his forces, when foreigners entered his gates and cast lots for Jerusalem—even you were as one of them" (v. 11). When the sides were drawn and attendance was taken, Edom (like Judas Iscariot on the night of Jesus' betrayal) was found in the company of God's enemies.

- *Envy can cause one to rejoice in the distress of another, something which truly incurs God's wrath.*

  "But you should not have gazed on the day of your brother in the day of his captivity; nor should you have rejoiced over the children of Judah in the day of their destruction" (v. 12).

- *Envy can cause one to plunder another's sphere, convinced that the other's possessions or domain are one's due.*

  "You should not have entered the gate of My people in the day of their calamity. Indeed, you should not have gazed on their affliction in the day of their calamity, nor laid hands on their substance in the day of their calamity" (v. 13). Jacob had gained blessing from God seemingly by tricking Esau; now Edom felt that Israel's blessing was his rightful portion to confiscate. Envy had driven Edom to wrong conclusions.

- *Envy always backfires.*

  "For the day of the LORD upon all the nations is near;

as you have done, it shall be done to you; your reprisal shall return upon your own head" (v. 15). Convinced they were wronged, Edom had taken revenge on Israel. Now, because of God's judgment, others would come and exercise revenge upon them. Edom's violence returned on his own head.

• *In the end, the one who envies will lose his inheritance to the one he envied.*

"The South shall possess the mountains of Esau" (v. 19). Even though Esau envied Jacob and even plundered him, the Lord said that in the end Edom's mountains would become the dominion of Israel.

THE VENOM OF DELAY

The principles found in the book of Obadiah regarding envy are gripping in their implications. And now, as we return to the story of Israel's tedious detour around the land of Edom, we will see how God couldn't give Israel his inheritance without first dealing with Edom's envy.

The huge detour around the land of Edom was a desert path with no food or water in the natural habitat. When God led the people of Israel on this lengthy bunny trail, they didn't understand God's purposes, so they weren't exactly grateful. Their nasty attitudes and the attending consequences are recorded for us:

> Then they journeyed from Mount Hor by the Way of the Red Sea, to go around the land of Edom; and the soul of the people became very discouraged on the way. And the people spoke against God and against Moses: "Why have you brought us up out of Egypt to die in the wilderness? For there is no food and no water, and our soul loathes

this worthless bread." So the LORD sent fiery serpents among the people, and they bit the people; and many of the people of Israel died. Therefore the people came to Moses, and said, "We have sinned, for we have spoken against the LORD and against you; pray to the LORD that He take away the serpents from us." So Moses prayed for the people. Then the LORD said to Moses, "Make a fiery serpent, and set it on a pole; and it shall be that everyone who is bitten, when he looks at it, shall live." So Moses made a bronze serpent, and put it on a pole; and so it was, if a serpent had bitten anyone, when he looked at the bronze serpent, he lived (Numbers 21:4-9).

God knew that because of the lengthy delay the soul of the Israelites would become "very discouraged on the way." God was not upset at their discouragement but, rather, at how they chose to express it. He wanted to root out their ambition and to deal with Edom's envy, but their response was to complain. So God sent poisonous vipers into the camp to show them that their response to His dealings was literally killing them.

The New Testament gives us an interesting perspective on this story, telling us that the people perished from the serpent bites because they tempted Christ (see 1 Corinthians 10:9). They thought that the whole detour idea was dumb. They had stepped into the fruitful crescent of Canaan and now found themselves back in the wilderness without food and water—except for the manna they loathed by now. No doubt they were saying things like, "This is a stupid route to Canaan. God, do You know what You're doing? Man, even I could chart a better course than this!" They were tempting Christ by despising their provision of manna and accusing God's judgment and wisdom. Christ had shown His faithfulness to them countless times before, but now they were once again caught in the grip

The Envy Detour: Death or Destiny   123

of unbelief. Through their impatience they were actually striking out at God with their tongues.

In sending the serpents, God was basically saying, "Let me show you what you're doing. Let me illustrate it with some venomous serpents. They will strike out at you with their tongues and will poison you with their bitter venom. Perhaps they will help you to see that you have been poisoned by bitterness. They will do to you as you have done to Me. You have been bitten with bitter unbelief and it's killing you on the inside."

DEATH OR DESTINY?

God's delays have a purpose, but the season of delay is a time when we are especially tired, tender and vulnerable to temptation. If we do not guard our hearts and keep our carnal responses in check, we can run the risk of becoming a casualty.

When God takes you on a lengthy detour, you will be vulnerable to many possible venomous temptations that have the potential to leave a deadly bite: bitterness against God, unbelief (which is always the main one), carnal comparisons, backbiting, self-indulgence, complaining, accusing others, accusing God, and more.

GOD's deLays have a purpose; but the
season of deLay is a time when
we are especially tired, tender and
vulnerable to temptation.

The sobering point of the story is this: Not everyone survives the detour. Some are casualties. Think of it—you've come through the Red Sea, defeated the Amalekites, heard the voice of God at the mountain and survived 39 torturous years of wandering in the wilderness. When thousands of others were killed because of God's judgments, you remained. And now, just a few short months before entering Canaan you become a casualty! Have you come this far, dear saint, to get sidelined by weariness when the end of the race is almost in sight?

tHe sobeRING poINt of tHe stoRY is tHis: Not everyone suRvives tHe detouR.

Unfortunately for many during one of God's detours, people don't discern that God is wanting to deal with the ambitious, competitive spirit that has a sinister hold on their hearts. Most don't even realize it's a problem. God uses the delay to frustrate their personal agendas. The question is, Will they perceive that their frustration is the fruit of an ambitious spirit?

It's interesting to note that it's not the enemy that's knocking them off right now. When it comes to the enemy in Canaan, they're experiencing victories. But they're getting eaten alive by the issues in their own hearts.

Those who pass the detour test will find it opens to a doorway of spiritual destiny. Those who succumb to unbelief and discouragement will perish. The stakes are enormous! So thanks be to God that in the midst of the judgment, His mercy extends powerfully to His people and He provides a means of healing to those who have taken the bite. He is so merciful! Even here, those who have been bitten with the venom of ambition find mercy and restoration in the life-giving power of God's salvation. The serpent on the pole represents Christ, to whom we look today for healing from the deadly sting of envy, ambition and competition. He is such a good God! He has provided for our healing so that we might share in the glorious conquest of our promised land.

PURPOSE OF THE DETOUR

Let's summarize the benefits of the detour:

1. It dealt with Edom's envy. When Edom saw the agonizing road that Israel took to circumvent their land,
   trudging dispiritedly through a land with no water,
   their envy turned to pity. They saw how much Israel
   had to suffer just to honor Edom's borders. When
   Israel finally conquered Canaan, Edom's attitude was
   "Let them have it."
2. Israel ended up with a larger inheritance than initial-
   ly anticipated. The detour meant that they would
   have to conquer Amorite country first, before tackling
   Canaan. In the end, they got Canaan plus the land of
   the Amorites east of the Jordan. If they hadn't taken
   the detour, it's unlikely they would have ever challenged those other nations. It didn't feel like it at the
   time; but through the detour, God was showing them
   that He was *for* them.
3. It dealt with ambition in Israel. If Edom was envious
   toward Israel, it could certainly be said that Israel had
   a competitive spirit toward Edom. The detour around
   Edom was surfacing the ambitions of their own hearts.
   God was targeting this ancient rivalry with a finely
   crafted detour. The brother with the lesser inheritance
   will always envy the brother with the greater inheritance. The brother with the greater inheritance will
   always have to deal with a spirit of competition toward
   the brother with the lesser inheritance. Actually, all
   of us have to deal in some measure with both attitudes. All of us have a little of both Edom and Israel in
   us. We all have to deal with envy toward those who are

promoted over us, and with ambition when we're promoted over others.

RELEVANCE FOR TODAY

The story of Israel's long detour around Moab, and the attending snakebites, is intensely relevant to where the church is today.
Israel represents the brother (church/ministry) with the greater
inheritance; Edom represents the brother (church/ministry)
with the lesser inheritance. (God chooses our inheritance for us,
and it's different for each leader, church or ministry.) Then,
when God places these churches in the same community or
region, the relational dynamics are multitiered and extremely
intricate.

GOD NEVER makes the pathway to
greater fruitfulness enviable.

In these days, the Lord is taking certain members of His
church (usually those with the greater inheritance) through
detours and delays. But God has a purpose in not allowing you
to enter your inheritance the easy way. God wants to bless you
with your full inheritance, but He can only do that by dealing
with the envy of your brothers. He is going to make your path
pitiable before them. God never makes the pathway to greater
fruitfulness enviable. It always comes at a price that doesn't produce envy but instead produces a holy fear at the consecration
that fruitfulness exacts.

Paul spoke of it in these terms: "For I think that God has dis-
played us, the apostles, last, as men condemned to death; for we
have been made a spectacle to the world, both to angels and to
men" (1 Corinthians 4:9). Paul is saying, "Everybody is looking

at us and wondering what God is doing with us! Even the angels are looking at our path and scratching their heads." Perhaps Paul felt like that serpent impaled on the pole—a gazingstock for others to gawk at and wonder about, and draw premature opinions about. "What is God doing with *that* church?" "I wonder what's up with *his* ministry?" This is God's purpose, to make you a gazingstock. But as you persevere in discipline and temperance, one day your journey will become a life-giving source of encouragement to others who will walk a similar path.

A PERSONAL STORY

Most every pastor has an envy story to tell. But since I'm the one writing this book, I get to tell my story. My purpose in telling it is to illustrate through some of my own experience the principles of this chapter.

My first pastorate was in a tiny city in western New York State. I was 29 when I accepted the pastorate of this small, struggling church. My wife and I were young, eager, sincere and inexperienced; and we had many dreams. One of the first things I did was join myself to a prayer gathering of pastors from three other area churches that were in our same general stream. I wasn't prepared, however, for everything I would encounter.

One of the first things I learned was that these pastors all had a problem with a certain large, thriving church in our region. This large church had attracted sheep from virtually every other church in the region and had made no attempts to communicate with these pastors who had lost members. These pastors were charging the large church with being unethical, isolationistic and harboring sheep who had huge unresolved issues in their lives. Conversation in our pastoral prayer gatherings often reflected on this other church. The group definitely had an "us versus them" flavor, and I was expected to side with "us."

I was too inexperienced to know and discern envy accurately, but to me the whole thing wasn't adding up. If you put all four of our churches together, our combined attendance wasn't even a quarter of the large church's attendance. And the report I heard from sheep who attended the large church was that there were green pastures and still waters to be found there. So I decided to check it out for myself. I made an appointment and went to visit the pastor in his office.

His guard was up and he was ready for me. Previous visits from area pastors had been unpleasant for him and he was braced for more of the same. But I had come simply to meet him and hear his heart. My first visit told me there was a rich spiritual deposit in this brother and that I could learn a lot from him. So I came back to visit him again. By my third visit, he realized I was sincere in my desire for fellowship and our friendship began to build.

I once asked him, "Why don't you call the pastor when a family comes to your church from another church?" He said, "These pastors are envious enough of us as is; if I drew attention to the situation every time it happened, it would be all the worse. Furthermore, I simply don't have time to make all those phone calls." He said they had never done anything to draw people away from another church. All they had done was concentrate on providing rich feed for their flock. As a result, sheep would come from all over to be fed. I was fascinated by his pastoral philosophy and set my heart to be open and teachable.

As the months progressed, the blessing of the Lord began to fall upon our little church. Soon, our church wasn't so little anymore. It wasn't long before our church outgrew the other churches represented by the pastors of our prayer group. When that happened, the nature of my relationship with the other pastors curiously began to change.

The bottom line was this: People were now leaving their churches and coming to ours. I quickly discovered this was the giant stumbling block of interchurch relationships, the great downside to church growth, the nemesis of citywide unity. When a family made the transition from another church to ours, part of me rejoiced at having more hands in the field to help with the harvest, but part of me cringed at how I would walk the thing out with my pastor-friend from the church the people had left. In my years as a pastor I struggled to find an effective way to walk this dynamic out with my fellow pastors. When their insecurities produced envious responses, there seemed to be no right way to smooth over the bumps.

We grew to three weekend services and knew we had to get into a larger facility. The Lord provided land in a sovereign way, and we began to draft plans to build a new worship facility. It was to be one of the largest sanctuaries in our city. The Lord put it in our hearts to build on a cash basis only, without taking out any kind of mortgage on the new building. Once we were in the new facility, this would be a great blessing; but getting into the facility on cash only would be a great faith challenge.

Our congregation began to give sacrificially. But even though they were giving generously according to their ability, we weren't bringing in much more than 10 percent of the needed funds per year. Was it going to take us 8 to 10 years to occupy the new facility? Being in multiple services every weekend, the journey before us seemed interminable! After four years of sacrificial giving we hit a lull where it seemed all our momentum was gone. Financial giving trickled slower than ever. The pastoral staff was weary. The people were tired, and enthusiasm was low.

I began to ask, "How long, Lord?" I sought the Lord in prayer for understanding into the tedium of the journey. We were taking a laborious detour and I didn't understand why. I shared our plight with the other pastors of our area. They began to pray with us and for us. Then they began to inquire into our welfare and express things like, "We're sure hoping the Lord sends a major gift your way!" A couple area churches even gave offerings into our building fund!

Through that long delay and other refining circumstances in my life, the Lord was crushing me as a pastor. Through the crushing, He began to reveal to me how I had operated in an ambitious spirit in relation to the other pastors of the area. That element was such a tiny percentage of my motivation that for years I honestly hadn't seen it. But through the crushing, God was surfacing all kinds of issues in my life that He wanted me to deal with. Even though it was maybe less than 1 percent of what motivated me, I was shown how a little leaven leavens the whole lump, and this tiny fraction of ambition was in fact discoloring every aspect of my ministry.

So I called the regional pastors together for a special meeting and said, "The Lord has been revealing the motives of my heart, and now I see that I have actually related to you brothers in a spirit of rivalry. Something inside me has been ambitious to build my own ministry, and it has caused me to relate to you in a competitive way." They looked at me and said, "Yes. We know." I said to them, "Please pray for me." So I knelt before them and they laid their hands on me and prayed for me.

What a crushing experience that was for me! All I could do was humble myself under the mighty hand of God. As I reflect on it now, even though the detour was grueling in all that it surfaced, I'm thankful that the Lord loved me enough to use it in my life for refining and perfecting.

Through it all, I began to see the Lord's wisdom in taking us the long route. Not only had He dealt with issues in our hearts, but I saw that if we had moved into our new facility quickly and with ease, the temptation for envy would have been strong in the other churches of the area. If envy had erupted, even though the new facility would have been a blessing to us in our local church, an eruption of envy in the regional church would have been deadly to the purposes of God for our area. It would have been one step forward but two steps back. But because the Lord took us on an agonizingly slow detour, the other churches eventually became our cheerleaders.

When we finally took occupancy of the new building six and one-half years after purchasing the property, they all rejoiced with us at the goodness of God. And yes, the Lord did send along some large gifts at the very end which enabled us to get into the building sooner than we thought—and on cash only. But by the time we moved in, the envy factor had been dealt with by the Lord's wisdom, issues of ambition within us had been crushed severely by the Lord, and we were able to occupy a larger facility accompanied by the celebrations of the other brothers of the region.

> Oh, the depth of the riches both of the wisdom and knowledge of God! How unsearchable are His judgments and His ways past finding out! . . . For of Him and through Him and to Him are all things, to whom be glory forever. Amen" (Romans 11:33-36).

Chapter 9

Rooted in Love

If we were to admit it, all of us are in an identity crisis of sorts. That's why there's so much envy everywhere. Envy cannot find a hold on the heart of the saint who is fully established in his identity in the love of God.

> That Christ may dwell in your hearts through faith; that you, being rooted and grounded in love, may be able to comprehend with all the saints what is the width and length and depth and height—to know the love of Christ which passes knowledge; that you may be filled with all the fullness of God (Ephesians 3:17-19).

When we are rooted, grounded and perfected in love, our sense of identity in God is so profoundly fulfilled that nothing we see with the natural eye can produce an envious response within us. We wish for nothing that anyone else has because we already have everything there is to have—an extravagant, intimate relationship with the Lord of the universe!

I speak in theoretical terms, for I have not yet attained that fullness. Therefore, I'm still in something of an identity crisis myself. I am not yet "perfect in love" (1 John 4:18). For me to claim that I am *not* in an identity crisis would be to claim that I have entered into perfect love, and I have not. But I'm not discouraged; grace is abounding to me and I am entering into more and more of Christ's perfect love!

envy campaigns for one's placement; Love campaigns for the advancement of another.

The issue of envy boils down to love. "Love does not envy" (1 Corinthians 13:4). Because Jesus' love is totally selfless, our love for one another must also be selfless: "This is My commandment, that you love one another as I have loved you" (John 15:12).

Envy is inherently self-seeking, and thus it is not of love. Love embodies everything that envy is not. Envy campaigns for one's placement; love campaigns for the advancement of another. "As I have loved you"—what a word! As we abide in His love, surely all envy will be squeezed out, to be displaced by the limitless expanse of Christ's self-emptying love that is poured forth in our hearts by the Holy Spirit.

When I am rooted in the love of Christ and am entering into the knowledge of the vast dimensions (width, length, depth, height) of Christ's love, I make a fascinating discovery: It's in the knowledge of God that I discover who I am! When I come to know Him, He reveals to me what I look like to Him. When I realize what I look like to God—that He is ravished over my weak heart that pants for Him—then I find the courage to believe that I am who He says I am.

I envy others because I'm not fully content with who I am. And if I'm not happy with who I am, I still lack revelation of who I have been made in Christ. I am still not rooted and perfected in love. So, to put the final nail in envy's coffin, we must pursue the knowledge of the love of Christ.

"But the knowledge of the love of God is a lifetime pursuit that is never exhausted!" you might complain. Exactly so! That's why I'm not discouraged when I see envy creeping up in my heart again. I just die to self one more time and press my face into the cross of Christ. I have prepared myself to deal with the envy issue for the rest of my life. I may never attain uncontested victory in this life, but I do expect my level of victory to continually increase as I abide in His grace. Although I haven't conquered envy, I've learned to recognize it better. I've become a faster repenter. The best way to get on with God is to learn to become a professional repenter (i.e., *eager* repenter) in the courts of the Lord.

Instead of being jealous of another's attainments, we'll become jealous for another's attainments.

When the love of Christ captures our hearts, it fills us with a holy jealousy for the maturity of the bride (see 2 Corinthians 11:2). Here's how God's love will change our hearts: Instead of being jealous *of* another's attainments, we'll become jealous *for* another's attainments. We'll experience the inverse of envy. As long as envy binds our hearts, our sphere will be limited; but when a godly jealousy for the advancement of the bride's maturity grips our hearts, we will be granted by her Lord the awesome privilege and entrustment of serving her in humility and faithfulness.

OUR SOURCE OF IDENTITY

For many years I found a lot of my identity in my position and success as a minister of the gospel. I didn't realize it at the time, of course, but looking back now I can see it. As a young pastor of a thriving church, I was like the king in the proverb:

> There are three things which are majestic in pace, yes, four which are stately in walk: A lion, which is mighty among beasts and does not turn away from any; a greyhound, a male goat also, and a king whose troops are with him (Proverbs 30:29-31).

The "troops" in my congregation were increasing numerically and I was honored to serve them. Appearances suggested that my spiritual authority was growing because my following was growing. I don't think people would have commonly thought of me as cocky or arrogant, but I did enjoy the prestige of pastoring one of the larger churches in my circle of friends.

Then the mighty hand of God came into my life. (At my invitation, I might add. You know, we ask God for things without knowing what we're really asking for.) "If you endure chastening, God deals with you as with sons; for what son is there whom a father does not chasten?" (Hebrews 12:7). When God chastened my life, He shut down my ministry, sent me into the wilderness and eventually removed me from the pastorate as well. I lost all titles and positions I had ever held.

So now I'm in the identity crisis of my life. I have no position in my home church; I have no title before my name nor letters after my name; I have no team I'm leading; I have no troops

following. (All of this has been because of the debilitating physical injury mentioned in chapter 6.) I have struggled to process a
host of sorrowful emotions and painful losses while at the same
time finding myself enriched with something far greater—the
knowledge of the love of Christ. The pain of my losses has been
very real, but of even greater substance has been the enrichment
of Christ's revelations to my heart. Because of my identity crisis,
I have been particularly vulnerable to envy. And yet the grace of
God has been abundant to me in the journey, empowering me
with the love that will calm all of envy's storms.

I can only tell you of my pursuit. I am chasing after such a
filling, thrilling, electrifying relationship with the Lover of my
soul that my sense of identity is found in nothing else but who
I am in Christ and who He is in me! Like John the Baptist, I want
to be "great in the sight of the Lord" (Luke 1:15), not in the sight
of men—and all because I've come to a place of peace in who I am
before the throne of God. The key is found in living for an audience of One, a life lived before God instead of men. I'm asking
God that the carnal ambitions within my soul for recognition
among men might be redirected into an ambitious pursuit of
greatness among the hosts of heaven. The question is not, Who
am I on Earth? but, Who am I before the throne of God?

I stand before God as a king and a priest (see Revelation 1:6).
As a priest I minister to the King in the presence of His glory; as
a king I serve as one who helps to enforce the ever-increasing rule
of His kingdom in the hearts of men. This is who I am—and this
is who you are. There is no jockeying for position, for we all
share equally the same standing before God. Envy will lose all of
its power in our midst when the body of Christ rises to the
understanding of its position before God's throne. Before the
Father I am a son; before the Son I am a bride. The knowledge of
my identity in Christ produces a great depth of contentment in
my spirit and a fearless boldness in my soul. The passionately

burning affections of God have won me to His heart, and now I am released from the baggage that once caused me to determine my identity based upon comparing myself to other people. The knowledge of Christ is setting me free (see John 8:32).

It's in the beholding of Christ that we're able to see ourselves for who we really are. John wrote it this way: "We know that when He is revealed, we shall be like Him, for we shall see Him as He is" (1 John 3:2). The more I see Him, the more I understand who I am. When I see Him face-to-face, then I will know the fullness of who I am. Until that moment of full revelation, I will always lack understanding of the fullness of who I am. The degree to which I search to know Christ's love is the measure to which I will search to know my own identity. And to the degree that I struggle with an identity crisis is the measure to which I am vulnerable to the ravages of envy. Therefore, the best antidote to envy is the pursuit of the knowledge of the love of Christ. While it's true that my sense of identity will never be fully complete until I see Him face-to-face, the more I behold Him by faith, the freer I become.

I have determined to receive God's promise to Abraham as my own: "I am your shield, your exceedingly great reward" (Genesis 15:1). God is my reward. At the end of the day I get God! So I am already incredibly wealthy beyond description. No one can add anything to me because I already have everything— God Himself. There's not a soul on Earth who has anything to add to what God has already given me. My brothers and sisters in Christ play a powerful role in my life, however, in helping me to discover and understand the fullness of what has already been made mine. I do not need to strive to become successful because I already am a success—I have received the lavish love of Christ and am now a child of God. I am the richest that a human being can become. But since my knowledge is limited, I continue to pursue the knowledge of God in Christ Jesus.

Please do not suppose me to be advocating an isolationistic individualism that would separate one from the rest of the body of Christ. We need each other! Ephesians 3:18 makes it very clear that the comprehension of the love of Christ is possible only within the communion of "all the saints." No solitary person can possibly exhaust the understanding of the love of Christ. At our best we can explore a tiny sliver of that love and pursue it all of our lives to its glorious limits. This is why we need the entire body for the love of Christ to be manifest. When we each bring the fruits of our lifelong pursuits to the table, we begin to see the immensity of the love of Christ. Rather than envying what another has uncovered of this wonderful love, I bask in it, for that person's pursuit has now enriched my life.

A False Source of Identity

God has created us with the need to know who we are. The longing for a solid self-identity is not sinful, but the way we pursue it can be sinful. Gaining our identity from what we do or what we possess never fills the void of the human spirit. The only thing that satisfies that void is an affectionate relationship with our Creator. It's knowing who we are in the arms of our beloved Bridegroom that establishes us in our true identity before God. When He whispers His intentions to us in the secret place, assuring us of His affections and declaring who we are in Him, He is establishing our hearts in grace. If, on the other hand, we try to fill our inner longings with success or position or stuff, we'll always come back to a nagging emptiness. And it's that emptiness that breeds competitiveness in the body of Christ and makes us susceptible to envy. Just look at King Saul's life.

I understand from personal experience the trap of finding my sense of identity from my accomplishments and successes. The reason I call it a trap is because it is the rare individual who has an unbroken line of successes in his history. For most of us, downturns inevitably come. When our identity is founded upon our performance, then we are set up for a crash landing. In good times we'll feel good about ourselves; in tough times we'll be down on ourselves. The tyranny of this kind of emotional roller-coaster ride makes us vulnerable to the ravages of envy. When my performance plummets, and with it my identity, then I begin to look at my brother's successes with an evil eye.

The Lord is teaching me that my sense of success is to be found in His presence. When I am relating to Him in abandoned love, I am successful. Period. You might ask, "What can I do to find my identity in Christ?" For me, the answer is to be found in my "secret place" relationship with God. (I share my heart on this subject in my book *Secrets of the Secret Place*.) As I meditate in the truth of His Word and allow the Holy Spirit to personalize His truth to my heart, I begin to burn with fiery zeal because I am finding ownership of His truth as it applies to my life. The Holy Spirit helps me to believe the love of Christ for me, which is the most liberating revelation to be gained in the universe.

I have discovered it's possible to be successful before men but barren before God.

Ministry accomplishments can deceive me into thinking they are the measure of God's approval on my life. I have discovered it's possible to be successful before men but barren before God. There is a place in God where I really can gain my sense of identity and fulfillment by worshiping Him and gazing upon His face. I've caught a glimpse of it, and I'm after it with all my heart.

When my sense of personal identity is founded upon the rock of Christ's love for me, I am secure in my identity because

Christ's love is unconditional, having no connection whatsoever to my ministry performance. Even when my ministry is soaring and the anointing is breaking yokes of bondage in the lives of others, His love remains constant in its fullness. God wants us to make the transition from finding our identity in our giftings to finding our identity in His love. I am His child, hidden with Christ in God, seated with Christ in heavenly places, overcoming the world. I am one who stands in His presence and gazes upon His face. That's who I am and that's what I do. And no person or crisis can strip me of this identity.

It was Jesus' knowledge of who He was that empowered Him to serve others selflessly (see John 13:3-5). It's the same way for me. When I know where I've come from and where I'm going to—in other words, when I know who I am—I can serve in the most menial ways because I am secure in my identity. One of the most powerful deterrents to envy is to pick up the servant's towel and wash the feet of others by serving their needs.

A personal friend, Pastor Michael Cavanaugh, told me how he chose to deal aggressively with a slight tinge of envy he was sensing. At the time, Michael and I were pastors of different churches in two communities separated by about 15 miles. Both of our churches were healthy and growing, and both were in the process of building new sanctuaries. However, our church had started building before theirs. At the time, it seemed to my friend Michael that we were always just one step in front of them.

Over time he began to feel that he was discerning small hints of competition between our ministries. He wasn't sure if the competition was in us toward them or in them toward us, but he decided to do something about it. What did he do? He wrapped himself in the servant's towel. He and his church elders decided to take *all the tithes* given to their church on a specific Sunday morning, designate them for our new building program and send the lump sum over to our church.

When their church members learned of the plan, they gave an above-average offering that Sunday morning. You could imagine our surprise when, upon opening our mail that week, we saw a check for almost $14,000! We were blown out of the water in gratefulness to God and in amazement over the generosity of the saints. Suffice it to say, that act of servanthood was a beautiful cure for any vestiges of competition and envy that might have wanted to lurk between our ministries.

sometimes it's tempting to think that a certain person or group is holding us back from our potential in Christ. but no one can deter you from pursuing the glorious Love of Christ!

After we were in our new building, our church responded in a similar gesture toward their church. Thus our mutual love and loyalty to each other was enhanced.

When I'm rooted in love, then promotion and demotion will both feel more and more the same to me. When I comprehend the love of Christ for me, then promotion on the human level appears more weak and temporary to me because I'm accurately discerning the essence of its vanity. And at the same time, demotion loses its sting because my confidence before God is not affected by the downturns of this human existence. What really matters is having the power of God's love stirring and moving my heart with burning affections. It's here, in this love, that envy is dissipated and true revivals of historic proportions are birthed.

No one else can hinder your pursuit of the upward call of God in Christ Jesus. Sometimes it's tempting to think that a certain person or group is holding us back from our potential in Christ. But no one can deter you from pursuing the glorious love of Christ! No one can slow down the pace of your pursuit when your heart is set on running the great race of faith and love. Even if your church shuts down your ministry, they cannot stop your hidden life in God. The pursuit of Christ's love sets us

> even if your church shuts down your ministry, they cannot stop your hidden Life in God.

free from the shackles that others might want to place on us, whether it be an unsaved spouse or a coworker or a church leader. The truth of this liberty will defuse any envy that might want to arise in our hearts.

In Summary

My prayer is that this book will give us the courage, whenever we feel the slightest pain over someone else's success, to admit our envy, be honest about it and bring it to the foot of the Cross. Instead of envying what God has given another, let's be thankful we're on the same team. While we all desire for the power and glory of God to be manifest in our generation, perhaps the most significant thing we can do to promote the furtherance of God's kingdom is to tear down the barriers of envy as soon as we see them in our hearts.

Instead of competing with and envying each other, let's celebrate what heaven has deposited in each other. Let's become jealous *for* the maturity of our brothers and sisters. As we perceive the measure of grace given to another, we are empowered to walk together in fellowship and unity. When I release you to function in your sphere, I am not jeopardizing my own sphere; rather, I am qualifying for greater fruitfulness in my own sphere.

This book is simply a call to walk in love. First, to believe and receive the great love God has for us; and then to reflect that love to our brothers and sisters. Oh, that we might be granted a revelation of the status God has given us in Christ Jesus before His throne! If we truly understood our identity in Christ, we would never envy again. The greatest antidote to envy is the pursuit of the knowledge of the love of Christ.

CALEB'S MOUNTAIN

I want to close with the story of a man in the Bible named Caleb. Caleb was one of the 12 spies who were sent into the land of Canaan to spy out the land when the people of God had freshly come out of Egypt. Caleb (together with Joshua) brought a good report to the people, that they were able with God's help to conquer the land of Canaan. Ten of the spies brought an evil report of unbelief, causing the nation to draw back in fear. The people decided they couldn't conquer Canaan, a decision that incurred upon them 40 years of wandering in the wilderness. Caleb and Joshua were consigned to wandering with the Israelites until the entire nation was ready to enter Canaan.

I always had this small, unspoken sentiment in the back of my mind, *God, I think it was cruel that you made Caleb and Joshua, who were ready to enter Canaan, wander for 40 years in the wilderness because of the other guys' unbelief.* But then the Lord began to show me the rest of the story.

When you get to the end of Caleb's life, you see that Caleb wound up inheriting an entire mountain in Canaan (see Joshua 14:6-15). When everyone else was being given a house in a field, Caleb was given a whole mountain.

When Caleb had to turn away from Canaan the first time and face the wilderness, I can imagine God saying, "Caleb, I love you so much in your stand of faith and loyalty to me, I tell you

what. I don't want to give you just a house in a field, like everybody else. I want to give you a greater inheritance because of
your faith and love; I want to give you an entire mountain. But
if I give you a mountain right now, you can't begin to imagine
the envy that would erupt in the nation. Everyone would have
a hissy fit on the spot! Everybody and their brother would
complain to the highest heaven about how unfair it is that you
should get a whole mountain, just because you're a man of faith.
So here's what we'll do to take care of the envy issue. If you'll
walk faithfully before Me for 40 years in the wilderness with My
people, I'll keep you strong and provide for you, and then I'll
bring you into the land. By enduring patiently for 40 years with
My chosen ones, you will gain the credibility before the entire
nation that is necessary if you are to ask for a mountain."

GOD GIVE US SPIRITUAL FATHERS
WHO HAVE PAID THE PRICE OF ENDURING
THROUGH THE WILDERNESS UNTIL
THEY'VE GAINED THE AUTHORITY BEFORE GOD
AND THE CREDIBILITY WITH MAN TO
ASK FOR AND TO TAKE AN ENTIRE MOUNTAIN
IN THE GRACE OF GOD.

When Caleb finally did ask for his mountain, nobody complained. Nobody said, "But hey, I'm only getting a house in a
field!" Everybody in the nation said, "Caleb wants a mountain?
Give him a mountain! He endured in faith for 40 years; so if anybody deserves it, Caleb does."

Caleb, through his faith and patience, ended up with such a
huge inheritance that he had enough to give not only to his sons
but also to his daughter, Achsah. She was rooted in her father's

love, so she said to herself, "My brothers have plenty, why shouldn't I ask my daddy for what I want too?" She asked, and he gave it to her. In fact, he gave her more than she asked for, giving her both the upper and lower springs (see Judges 1:15).

I've heard some sisters in the body of Christ complain, "They won't give me any inheritance in my church." Maybe it's because all that the brothers have is a house in a field and they have long since divvied that thing up in their minds, waiting for the father to kick the bucket. The sisters, they've long decided, aren't getting anything.

If the sisters are going to get a share of the inheritance, they need to have a rich daddy. My spirit says, God give us spiritual fathers who have paid the price of enduring through the wilderness until they've gained the authority before God and the credibility with man to ask for and to take an entire mountain in the grace of God. Then, like Caleb, they will have a sufficient spiritual inheritance to distribute to the sons and daughters alike.

When Papa gives it to you, nobody can argue, "But you're a sister; you shouldn't be doing that in the church!" The sister replies, "If you have a problem with me living in this territory, talk to Papa. He gave it to me." Nobody would question the father because they know he'll say, "Is it not lawful for me to do what I wish with my own things? Or is your eye evil because I am good?"

When the spiritual fathers give out the inheritance, the argument is over. And the brothers won't envy because they've got more than enough for themselves.

Also by Bob Sorge

Exploring Worship: A Practical Guide to Praise and Worship
> Used internationally as a text for local church worship teams and college worship classes, this is must reading for music ministers, worship leaders, musicians and worshipers. Both devotional and practical in nature.

Exploring Worship Workbook and Discussion Guide
> Written in short answer and fill-in-the-blank style, this companion study guide helps small groups work systematically through *Exploring Worship*.

In His Face: A Prophetic Call to Renewed Focus
> This is an intense book that calls us back to the centrality of a moment-by-moment walk with Jesus. Through gentle instruction, urgent warning and heartwarming insight, Bob will rekindle your passion for Jesus.

The Fire of Delayed Answers
> Written from the author's own crucible, this spiritual food for those in crisis helps to clarify why the answers to our prayers may be delayed and also gives practical advice for walking in faith and hope until God's release comes.

The Fire of God's Love
> The passion of Christ's cross is an extravagant invitation to the blazing inferno of His love. Listen as the Lord Jesus draws you into an intensity of love that burns away every competing affection.

*Pain, Perplexity and Promotion: A Prophetic Interpretation
of the Book of Job*

This may be the most heartfelt and relevant look at the
book of Job that you'll ever read. Job's journey is a pattern for how God takes a blameless man with a willing
spirit and promotes him to a higher spiritual plane than
he could have ever imagined.

Dealing with the Rejection and Praise of Man

Rejection and praise are like twin gulleys that flank the
highway of holiness. Learn how to hold your heart
before God in a way that pleases Him in the midst of
both rejection and praise from people.

Glory: When Heaven Invades Earth

You love the presence of God, but you'll never be satisfied until you see the glory of God. This book will renew
your hope for a full-blown explosion of God's glory in
the earth.

Secrets of the Secret Place

Bob shares some of the secrets he's learned in making
the secret place energizing and delightful. Readers everywhere are finding fresh momentum in their devotional
life with God. This is also a great resource for small
groups.

Bob Sorge's books may be ordered from your local bookstore or
directly from Oasis House:

Phone orders: 1-816-623-9050
Website orders (fully secure): www.oasishouse.net

More of the Best
from Bob Sorge

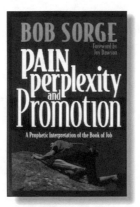

The Fire of Delayed Answers: Are You Waiting for Your Prayers to Be Answered?
Paperback
ISBN 09621.18532

Pain, Perplexity and Promotion: A Prophetic Interpretation of the Book of Job
Paperback
ISBN 09261.18567

Secrets of the Secret Place: Keys to Igniting Your Personal Time with God
Paperback
ISBN 09704.79107

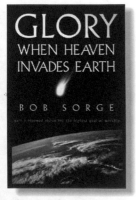

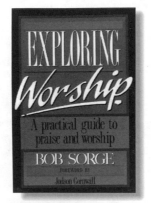

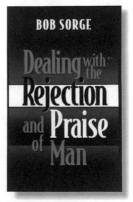

Glory: When Heaven Invades Earth
Paperback
ISBN 09621.18591

Exploring Worship Workbook (Study Guide)
Paperback
ISBN 09621.18516

Dealing with the Rejection and Praise of Man
Paperback
ISBN 09621.18583

Available at your local Christian bookstore.

Character Is a Compass for the Conscience

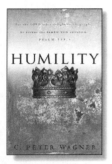

Humility
C. Peter Wagner
Hardcover
ISBN 08307.29356

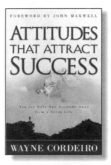

Attitudes That Attract Success
You're Only One Attitude
Away from a Great Life!
Wayne Cordeiro
Paperback
ISBN 08307.28880

Caring Enough to Confront
How to Understand and
Express Your Deepest
Feelings Toward Others
David Augsburger
Paperback
ISBN 08307.07336

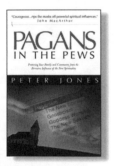

Pagans in the Pews
Protecting Your Home
and Family from the Pervasive
Influence of the New Spirituality
Peter Jones
Paperback
ISBN 08307.27981

Love, Acceptance and Forgiveness
Equipping the Church
to Be Truly Christian
in a Non-Christian World
*Jerry Cook and
Stanley C. Baldwin*
Paperback • ISBN 08307.06542

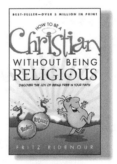

How to Be a Christian Without Being Religious
Discover the Joy of Being
Free in Your Faith: A User-
Friendly Study of Romans
Fritz Ridenour
Paperback
ISBN 08307.27892